“Take one step towards me,
I will take
ten steps
towards you.
Walk towards me,
I will run
towards you.”

HADITH QUDSI

PRAISE FOR *BIG LITTLE STEPS*

"*Big Little Steps* breaks down a woman's journey to Islam in big little pieces."

Grazia Middle East

"This is a book full of heart. New Muslims and those who are newly committed to their religion will find much useful information conveyed with common sense and compassion."

Ingrid Mattson*, PhD, London and Windsor Community Chair in Islamic Studies, Faculty of Theology, Huron University College.*

"*Big Little Steps* is a holistic and feminine take on the ins and outs of Islam, written by a young French lady. It is an easy to understand and useful guide to anyone wanting to become Muslim, especially those brave women! I wished I'd had a book like this when I embraced Islam in 1995."

Kristiane Backer*, author of 'From MTV to Mecca'.*

"*Big Little Steps* is a heart-warming journey of an intelligent woman seeking the peace of Allah. Full of practical advice and insightful thoughts, this is one book that every Muslimah should be talking about."

Quake Books

"A riveting read that reflects the author's first-hand experience as a Muslim convert woman (…) we promise you won't be able to put it down."

Harper's Bazaar*, Arabia.*

Mathilde Loujayne

Big Little steps

A Woman's Guide to Embracing Islam

Foreword by Dr. Myriam Francois

Big Little Steps: A Woman's Guide to Embracing Islam (Revised Edition)

First published in England by
Kube Publishing Ltd
Markfi eld Conference Centre
Ratby Lane, Markfi eld, Leicestershire
LE67 9SY United Kingdom
Tel: +44 (0) 1530 249230
Email: info@kubepublishing.com
Website: www.kubepublishing.com

5th impression, 2024.

Cataloguing-in-Publication Data is available from the British library

ISBN 978-1-84774-127-1 Paperback
ISBN 978-1-84774-128-8 ebook

Editor: Hannah Bass
Illustrator: Hatty Pedder
Watercolour Illustrations: Christine Shamsa
Cover and Interior Layout Design: Inna Vinchenko

English Language Worldwide Rights, excluding the Middle East, granted by The Dreamwork Collective, Dubai, UAE.

Printed by: Elma Basim, Türkiye

IN LOVING MEMORY OF MY BROTHER STÉPHANE.

I've missed you big bro, may your soul rest in peace. Love you to the moon and back.
"To God we belong, and to God we will return."[1]

TO MY PARENTS,

I can never thank you enough for your support, education, love and encouragement every step of the way, and for helping me believe in myself in anything I do. As my father says, *"Shoot for the moon and you'll land amongst the stars."* I love you both.

TO MY HUSBAND AND DAUGHTER,

You guys are my rock, you feed me with love and happiness on a daily basis. Maria, I hope you'll be inspired by this book to reach your fullest potential – once you get past the age of scribbling all over it!

SPECIAL THANKS TO:

Tasneem, Fouad, Kira and Salwa for taking on this challenge – I couldn't have done it without you. Samira, Allal, Sukayna, Eman, Salman and my mentor Sheikh Khalfan Al Esry (may your soul rest in peace) for your continuous spiritual support.

Peace and love to you all!

1. The Cow,
Surah Al Baqarah (2:156)

CONTENTS

FOREWORD

Big Little Steps landed on my bookshelf and immediately felt like an anomaly alongside the austere and serious tomes on Islamic jurisprudence and history gathering dust. A pastel shade of pink was the author's choice of colour for the cover, Loujayne says she designed it to be "feminine looking" to appeal to the female audience the book is geared towards. The author's ambition is to "highlight beautiful verses of the Quran, women's rights and accomplishments, break misconceptions and talk about taboos" in a relatable and 'light' style, in contrast with the laborious and heady feel of many books about Islam currently on the market. As is often the lament of new Muslims, finding an accessible, easy to read and friendly book on Islam was a struggle, and so Loujayne decided to take on the not so easy task herself.

She decided what was lacking was an informative, light read which could dispel misconception, while providing an overview of the faith and its central tenets and beliefs. Describing many of the books she'd read on Islam as "harsh and unrelatable," – and perhaps not coincidentally written by men – Mathilde weaves her own personal story of conversion to Islam, into this accessible manuscript in which personal anecdotes mix with more formalistic descriptions of religious practise, as well as, in some cases, more questionable attempts to establish a sense of religious orthodoxy. The latter point is perhaps what I felt less comfortable with, given the breadth of interpretation of the faith of 1.8 billion people, and also with regards to the objective of providing the reader with a means into the topic without sounding overly 'preachy'.

The US Personal Development Industry is currently (2018) worth $9.9 Billion – a portion of which reflects a real hunger for self-help, spiritual guidance and life advice books. While other religious denominations have so far produced a range of 'gurus' or spiritual guides who offer up ancient wisdom in bite size, digestable portions for an audience unaccustomed to the heady work of more traditional religious practise, Muslims have so far been largely absent from this market. Some might argue this isn't a bad thing, and it is worth questioning whether a watered down version of religious practise to suit the vagaries of the modern lifestyle is a worthy adaptation, but there is certainly an avid market of spiritually hungry consumers who may well savour this lighter offering.

Drawing on the growing market for 'self-help' books, Loujayne taps into a much underrepresented style within Islamic literature, a "self-help" book for Muslims, which seeks both to inspire Muslim women, but also to educate those outside the faith. This two pronged market approach, speaking to audiences with quite distinct needs, means the book moves between an insider conversation about what spiritual solutions Islam has to offer modern women in their search for a balanced lifestyle, and an educational text about the core beliefs of Muslims.

The book's strength lies in its attempt to provide an islamically grounded series of prescriptions for the modern ailments which the self-help market so lucratively targets – detoxing, physio-spiritual practise, natural remedies, fasting. As adepts of other spiritual traditions before her have done, Loujayne aims to provide distilled knowledge of the benefits of certain ritual, dietary and devotional practises within Islam to assist the busy, modern woman in her search for traditionally rooted remedies to many of our very modern ills. Critics of the self-help movement may question the scientific basis for some of these claims, but the genre is a growing one and a Muslim contribution seems overdue. Some may take issue with the adoption of individual practises outside of the broader framework of Islam, and yet the direction of religious practise in the West is towards a greater focus on spirituality and less focus on traditional structures.

Like many travellers on the road of spiritual practise, including many non-denominational practitioners, Loujayne and her family are seeking to draw on timeless recommendations within the Islamic tradition to help them navigate and in some cases resist the very contemporary ailments associated with advanced capitalism, namely the commodification of and an obsession with productive capacity. Those familiar with the self-help literature will recognise the call to lead a simpler life, more connected with the natural elements and more in tune with one's bodily and spiritual needs. And I have long felt that a religious tradition as rich as Islam was a glaring omission in the display of books offering helpful tips on dealing with everything from stress, to how to lead a cruelty free life. In this area, Loujayne makes good headway, although the book would have benefited from acknowledging that the views expressed are Loujayne's, not some expression of immutable orthodoxy.

In the second half of the book, Loujayne takes on some of the central critiques made about Muslims, specifically with regard to the treatment of women. Here, her accessible approach seeks to provide modern readings of historical female figures to counter the commonly wielded tropes about Islam's presumed misogynistic bent. Feminism, art, minimalism, an alternative vision of the role Muslim women can and have played historically is offered up to the reader, drawing on the sorts of references and language you're probably more used to reading in Grazia than any existing Islamic literature. Here again though, Loujayne's own interpretation can't be taken as orthodoxy, and future works in this genre would be enriched by a recognition of pluralism and diversity of perspectives. This second half of the book focuses in on some of the practises more common to the normative practise of the faith, while weaving aspects of Loujayne's personal story throughout. For those seeking a friendly and welcoming insight into some of the basic tenets and beliefs of the faith, Loujayne's book offers a welcome addition to a women's perspective on Islam and a much needed contribution to existing Islamic literature.

Dr. Myriam Francois

INTRODUCTION

EPIPHANY

2

In the name of God,
the Lord of Grace,
the Ever-Merciful

Quran, 1:1

"I hope there will be croissants in Paradise." Just reaching the office and not fully awake yet, I was daydreaming about the crunchy, buttery croissant I was enjoying at my desk before beginning my day. I'm a traditional French woman in most ways, so croissants are the way to go when I want to treat myself. When I posted this comment on my Facebook page, I didn't expect any kind of applause from my friends for my creativity, but I certainly wasn't expecting the reaction of an ex-colleague. Concerned about my comment, she wrote that I should be more careful about what I write, as she knew I was a Muslim and people might think I was becoming an extremist.

This is the reality of living as a Muslim these days: if you're vocal about anything that is remotely connected to your faith, you're labelled as extreme. As a white westerner who didn't wear a headscarf (although I still dressed modestly), you wouldn't have guessed I was Muslim. And yet, despite trying to blend in by not wearing my faith on my sleeve, these kinds of hurtful comments still came – and they slowly but surely drove me to hide my faith as a western Muslim for years, as many do. The effect was that I was living a lie; hiding from my true self. I have since met many other Muslim converts who describe themselves as 'in hiding'.

This book is an answer to all the people who have asked with a raised eyebrow and a hint of suspicion, "But why did you convert?" It's about the lessons I have learned and my personal advice to those discovering their faith or reconnecting with Islam, wanting to live their lives as practicing Muslims. Of course, I welcome anyone who is interested, Muslims and non-Muslims alike.

For parents whose children have embraced Islam, here is what my mum would tell you: she has never seen me more balanced; she has watched me grow into a kind, smart and loving human being. Stop worrying and start learning!

South of France, early 90s

God was never a part of my upbringing. In my family of Freemasons, everyone was atheist. It wasn't until I turned eight years old that I started to learn about the universe, which made me feel like a small ant among these infinite worlds. I asked myself, "Who created this?" and, "How am I here?" I was in a private elementary school in Marseilles and my questions were quickly answered: God.

Back then, most private schools in France were Catholic, so the nuns and the priest accompanied me in my journey as I started to attend Church. Despite not being religious themselves, my parents were very supportive of me getting baptised and attending after-school religious activities, like catechism lessons and field trips to monasteries. As far as I knew, I was the only person with faith in God in my family, which amused everybody.

But little did I know, my father had survived cancer before I was born and had started a spiritual journey of his own, finding answers as to what his purpose in life was. Around this time, he was saying his declaration of faith at a mosque in Marseilles. He didn't tell any of us, wanting to keep his choice private until he was ready.

Then, our whole world turned upside down. My older brother Stéphane passed away at the age of sixteen. From then on, my goal in life was to be reunited with him by becoming the best person I could be.

Sultanate of Oman, late 90s

Marseilles was too painful for our family after my brother passed, and my father began to search job opportunities in a Muslim country. He was given the opportunity to move to Muscat, the capital of Oman, and we leapt at the chance to move away from the pain and sorrow of our grief.

Here, in a land of sunshine and warm, welcoming people, we were given a new lease of life. I joined an international American school with more than fifty different nationalities among its students. I quickly found catechism lessons and like-minded friends who believed in God – they were Christians too, but Orthodox and Protestant. I was growing into a popular teenager, and we had fun jet-skiing, camping and partying – just like any regular school girl.

Around this time, it was revealed to me that my father had converted to Islam. Since the process had been years in the making, my mother wasn't surprised; in fact, she started to study the Quran herself, weeping as she read. My father explained that his experience with cancer in the 1980s had humbled him and led him to think about the 'bigger questions' of life. Having also read about Hinduism, Judaism and Christianity, he had found himself drawn to Islam.

My father started to take us with him to celebrate *Eid,* which was always a fun experience. Muslims were so friendly and welcoming and I never felt judged for being of a different faith. Rather, I enjoyed the perks of celebrating all holidays, meaning more presents! I also saw some of my friends fasting at school during Ramadan. Muslim or not, everyone blended in with this peaceful and respectful culture.

Finding my father's choice somewhat intriguing, I would debate religion at home with him and with my friends at school. My schoolmates and I would share our views on the Pope and on matters that affected teenagers, like sexual relationships, boyfriends, abortion, taking the pill... Their point of view was different to mine and it made me feel that I needed to be more open-minded and learn more about other religions.

Then, I found out that a revised edition of the Bible was being released. Until then, I had not realised that the original text had been modified over the centuries. Frustrated and determined to know the truth, I wanted to read the authentic words of God. I thought to myself, "How can I read the original book?"

September 11, 2001

We all remember where we were that day when we heard the breaking news. I also remember how all eyes turned to Muslims as the discrimination began. "What does this have to do with Islam?" I thought. "My dad is a Muslim and he would never do this. The country I live in is Islamic but no one I know would ever do this."

Since I had started to educate myself on other religions, specifically the Orthodox Church, I decided to jump right into the Quran to be able to understand what was happening in the world. Through my research into these ancient scriptures, I was also hoping to understand why my brother had been taken away from us at such a young age.

March 2002

When I was about halfway into reading the Holy Quran, I had what felt like an epiphany; I had unearthed a chest of treasures in which each gem further enlightened me to the truth. I had found the authentic word of God, the source of all things. I couldn't believe that Muslims also believed in Jesus as a Messenger of God, and that the Quran revealed what really happened to him.

This treasure boosted my faith in God, gave me more answers than I expected, helped me grieve, and unexpectedly brought me inner peace. I asked my high school librarian if she could help me become a Muslim and she introduced me to Sheikh Khalfan Al Esry, a famous Islamic scholar in Oman (may his soul rest in peace).

My parents and I spoke about my decision and they were supportive, so Sheikh Khalfan came over to our house and we sat at the dinner table with my cousin, who was visiting. He wanted to make sure I had the right intentions, that I was a balanced teenager, and he explained about the five pillars of Islam. These pillars would become the foundation that held my faith together. I pronounced my declaration of faith (the *shahada*) in both English and Arabic, declaring my belief that there is only one God and that Muhammad, Jesus, Moses and Abraham are His Messengers. I turned eighteen years old a few days later.

My twenties

My enthusiasm for my newfound religion was not shared by my Christian friends. I hadn't expected this backlash since I hadn't left my faith in God behind and I didn't feel any different. I didn't desert Christianity; rather, I felt that I had upgraded my faith and now had the latest version! Islam was the crystallisation: all the different pieces of my spirituality coming together.

I graduated from high school three months later and moved to Paris to study public relations at university. I decided this would mark a new beginning for me – it was a great opportunity to leave my reputation as a party girl behind! I would try to find other converts to become friends with and focus on my studies so that I could move back to a Muslim country as quickly as possible.

Islamophobia was growing globally and I told only a handful of new friends that I had converted to Islam. Some were supportive, others not. I remember once casually telling a new friend over the phone; she hung up on me! I was the only Muslim convert I knew at the time, and relevant content for new Muslims on the internet was scarce. I'm so grateful I had my father to talk to during that time. We'd stay up late talking about the Quran and other world religions for hours and hours.

When I converted, I had thought, "This is it. I've found the truth and I can rest on my laurels now." It wasn't until I found a job in Dubai, United Arab Emirates and moved back to the Middle East that I realised my conversion was only the beginning of a new journey. Up to this point, I had read the Quran from cover to cover several times and had progressively lost interest in drinking and partying. I was evolving without even noticing it – slowly but surely making big little steps and progressing. As the author Paulo Coelho once tweeted, "Life is a journey, not a race." Similarly, I realised that finding Islam was about living the journey, not reaching a destination.

In Dubai, I finally met other converts for the first time, and I realised that Islam was more than a faith – it was also a way of life (what Muslims call the *deen*). Meeting girls and women who had their own stories and reasons for embracing Islam was a joy and relief – I no longer felt like the odd one out and I didn't have to hide who I really was. We connected instantly and their individual stories never cease to amaze me.

My work then brought me to live in Toronto, Canada and Los Angeles, USA for a while, where I discovered Islamic centres and met amazing women walking the same big little steps. I realised we all had similar concerns – relationships, prayer, family… Islam became for me a tightknit community of sisters and brothers who instantly made me feel part of their family. I went from being the only Muslim convert I knew other than my dad, to entering a larger-than-life community called *ummah*.

Each new encounter made me feel less alone. As I attended classes I met many more sisters who shared my questions about Islamic education. Unfortunately, I never found a one-stop book for converts that addressed these questions while being appealing and easy enough to read.

So, in my mid-twenties, I decided to gather all those questions and write a guide based on my personal experiences that would help women around the world tackle these issues. I interviewed more than fifty women from different countries to understand what mattered to them most.

My thirties

One cosy evening I was chatting with my parents when my dad and I jokingly asked my mum if she was ready to become a Muslim like us. Needless to say, we didn't expect to hear that she wanted to say her pronunciation of faith with us! She had learned about Islam through living in Oman and through our conversions, and had long felt that the faith – and the way of life – resonated with her. She now says she doesn't know why she was afraid to take the leap earlier.

The morning after her conversion, my mum asked, "What does *Allahu Akbar* mean? I heard it all night long in my dreams."

With goosebumps, I told her, "It means 'God is the greatest.' The angels were welcoming you into Islam."

Although I now had a family of Muslims, finding a husband was like finding a needle in a haystack. I'm French but I had never met a French Muslim man, and I wanted to be with a Muslim; I'm Muslim but I am not Middle Eastern. Where was this man hiding?

I was about to give up on my dream man when at last I met my husband. Funnily enough, I was being interviewed for a documentary about Muslims and he was the cameraman! We now have a beautiful and funny daughter of our own. Together, we have been on several pilgrimages to Makkah and he encouraged me to write this book. I decided to quit my corporate job and make my dream come true.

What's your story?

This book is not about me: I've written it for you and to form a community of like-minded women. My story is merely one of many. So be your own soul-teacher – feel free to mark your personal comments and questions in the margins and to seek answers on your own.

I am not an Islamic scholar – I am a woman of faith with more than fifteen years of experience in the Muslim community. I have simply made the effort to dig deep into research to be sure I've made the right choice for myself. Now I want to pass on this knowledge, since Islam encourages us all to help each other.

As a Muslim, I am very aware of how our religion is sometimes negatively perceived, which is inflamed by those who choose to willingly, or ignorantly, distort Islamic teachings, and commit terrible acts of violence and oppression against women, non-Muslims or those deemed "not Muslim enough". However, I don't discuss this any further in the book as this is not what this book is about.

My mission is to share what I've learned over the years, backed up by beautiful verses from the Quran and narrations of the Prophet Muhammad (peace be upon him). I want to unearth what Muslim women have achieved in many fields over the centuries. I also want to shed light on the way women were treated before the Quran was revealed, and how ground-breaking Islam was. I want to share miracles found in the Quran and how it conveys to us a way of life that can help us heal from within.

I'll take you through a variety of topics that cover faith, well-being, community, women and, when you're ready, prayer.

Assuming that you might not be an Arabic speaker, I've kept all Islamic terminology in English rather than Arabic for a smooth reading experience. I've also included a glossary of the most commonly used terms and phrases for your convenience, and a list of my favourite books that I recommend you read if you want to carry on with your research. Every month, I discuss these in an online book club called 'Soul Sisters' on Goodreads, which you are welcome to join!

Additionally, it is customary for Muslims to wish peace and blessings upon all the Prophets, their wives and companions (may Allah be pleased with them) when we mention their names. However, for a better flow, I have only mentioned it at the beginning of the book. As you read through the chapters, I leave it up to you to wish blessings upon them out of respect.

Last but not least, I say a little prayer for you. I pray that God guides you on your journey, whatever it may be. What might seem like one small step for you may be one giant leap towards God's infinite love. As He reaches out to your heart, I ask you to open your mind.

I apologise if I've made any mistakes in this book; the truth is only with God, the All-Knower. I'm a student of Islam and will continue to learn from God, from our scholars, and from the lives of those who were grateful to their Creator.

I hope you enjoy reading and that you'll join me in building our community of soul sisters!

CHAPTER

1 FAITH

Kindness is a mark of faith, and whoever has no kindness has no faith.[1]

Prophet Mohammad

Love, hope, faith… can they be taught, faked and passed on to generations through our DNA? We are all born with a natural inclination, or perhaps a need, to believe, and eventually each one of us comes to a crossroad in our lives. Some of us choose to ignore the hint of faith that once sparked within, eventually losing sight of the question that crossed our minds: 'Does God exist?' Others walk away from the upbringing that they had never believed in. But what if they have given up their faith for the wrong belief?

For believers who have taken the leap of faith to believe in God, isn't choosing your religion the natural next step? If faith is not genetic then why on earth can't we question what we've been taught, debate society's mainstream school of thought and make sense of this great mystery that is religion? At the end of the day, it is human nature to want to believe, to have hopes and to dream, irrespective of colour and social status. I believe that only our Creator would instil this need in our souls, as a means to remember Him.

1. Hadith source: Muslim

What has faith meant to me before and after converting to Islam?

Faith is enlightenment, the ignitor of love, compassion and forgiveness that run through my veins, the light that makes me see the world differently and the answer to the question of my purpose in life. My faith also represents comfort for my heart, the healer of my grief and my 'chicken soup for the soul'. My journey started with questions from which my faith was born, but the path to finding the right practice for my spirituality was a long, winding road that finally led me to Islam. At every bend in the road stood a question, and another, until I reached clarity about who I was truly meant to be: a Muslim.

What does faith mean to you?

1. WHO IS GOD?

In Islam, God is referred to as Allah. Why? The Arabic word 'Allah' literally translates to 'The God' – 'the' emphasising that there is no other. While most Arabic nouns are either masculine or feminine, the noun 'Allah' has no gender and is always singular, never plural. Interestingly, 'Allah' isn't used exclusively by Muslims. In fact, Arab Christians and Jews also use 'Allah' in their scriptures, highlighting the similarity between the three monotheistic faiths.

Sometimes thinking about Allah can be daunting – He is so vast and beyond comprehension. Familiarising yourself with His names and thinking about their meanings is an effective way to get to know God and become closer to Him.

> "He is God: there is no deity other than Him. It is He who knows all that is beyond the reach of anyone's perception, as well as all that which can be witnessed. He is the Lord of Grace, the Ever-Merciful.
>
> He is God: there is no deity other than Him, the Sovereign, the Holy, the Source of Peace, the Giver of Faith, the Guardian over all, the Almighty, the Compeller, to whom all greatness belongs. Exalted is God in His limitless glory above anything they associate as partner with Him.
>
> He is God: the Creator, the Maker who gives shape and form to all. His are the most gracious names. Everything in the heavens and earth extols His limitless glory. He alone is the Almighty, the Wise."

The Exile - *Surah Al-Hashr* (59:22-24)

– GOD IS ONE –
He is the one and only God, He has no partner and no children.

– GOD IS UNIQUE –
He is the greatest, there are no greater or lesser gods.

– GOD IS ETERNAL –
He has existed since before the beginning of time and will exist beyond the end of time.

– GOD IS OMNISCIENT –
He is all-seeing and all-knowing. He knows everything that can be known and can do everything that can be done.
God is neither male nor female.

– GOD IS JUST –
He rewards and punishes fairly.
God is merciful and His mercy has no limits.

THE 99 NAMES AND

"His are the most gracious names."[1] Allah is just one of God's names in Islam. His names and attributes are mentioned throughout the Quran to depict His bounties and to describe Him. Those who learn them, ponder over them and contemplate them will be the closest to knowing God.

1. The Exile - *Surah Al-Hashr* (59:24)

	Arabic	Meaning	
1	الرحمن	The Most Gracious	*Ar-Rahman*
2	الرحيم	The Most Merciful	*Ar-Rahim*
3	الملك	The Sovereign	*Al-Malik*
4	القدوس	The Holy One	*Al-Quddus*
5	السلام	The Source/Giver of Peace	*As-Salam*
6	المؤمن	The Guardian of Faith/Giver of Security	*Al-Mu'min*
7	المهيمن	The Protector/Preserver of Safety	*Al-Muhaymin*
8	العزيز	The All-Mighty	*Al-Aziz*
9	الجبار	The Irresistible	*Al-Jabbar*
10	المتكبر	The Supreme	*Al-Mutakabbir*
11	الخالق	The Creator	*Al-Khaliq*
12	البارئ	The Inventor of All Things	*Al-Bari'*
13	المصور	The Shaper of Beauty	*Al-Musawwir*
14	الغفار	The Forgiving	*Al-Ghaffar*
15	القهار	The Subduer	*Al-Qahhar*
16	الوهاب	The Giver of All	*Al-Wahhab*
17	الرزاق	The Provider	*Ar-Razzaq*
18	الفتاح	The Opener	*Al-Fattah*
19	العليم	The All-Knower	*Al-`Alim*
20	القابض	The Constrictor	*Al-Qabid*
21	الباسط	The Reliever	*Al-Basit*

ATTRIBUTES OF ALLAH

Knowing God's characteristics will undeniably increase a believer's love for Him and can be very helpful in any situation in life. There is a famous saying in Islam: "And your Lord says: Call on Me, and I shall answer you…"[2] To call upon God by His attributes is the best way to praise Him!

2. The Forgiver *Surah Ghafir* (40:60)

Al-Khafid	The Abaser (of oppressors)	الخافض	22
Ar-Rafi	The Exalter	الرافع	23
Al-Mu'izz	The Bestower of Honours	المعز	24
Al-Mudhill	The Dishonourer	المذل	25
As-Sami	The All-Hearing	السميع	26
Al-Basir	The All-Seeing	البصير	27
Al-Hakam	The Judge	الحكم	28
Al-`Adl	The Just	العدل	29
Al-Latif	The Subtle One	اللطيف	30
Al-Khabir	The All-Aware	الخبير	31
Al-Halim	The Forbearing	الحليم	32
Al-Azim	The Magnificent	العظيم	33
Al-Ghafur	The Forgiver and Hider of Faults	الغفور	34
Ash-Shakur	The Rewarder of Thankfulness	الشكور	35
Al-Ali	The Highest	العلي	36
Al-Kabir	The Greatest	الكبير	37
Al-Hafiz	The Preserver	الحفيظ	38
Al-Muqit	The Nourisher	المقيت	39
Al-Hasib	The Accounter	الحسيب	40
Al-Jalil	The Mighty	الجليل	41
Al-Karim	The Generous	الكريم	42
Ar-Raqib	The Watchful One	الرقيب	43

	Arabic	Meaning	
44	المجيب	The Responder to Prayer	*Al-Mujib*
45	الواسع	The All-Comprehending	*Al-Wasi*
46	الحكيم	The All-Wise	*Al-Hakim*
47	الودود	The Loving One	*Al-Wadud*
48	المجيد	The Majestic One	*Al-Majid*
49	الباعث	The Resurrector	*Al-Ba'ith*
50	الشهيد	The Witness	*Ash-Shahid*
51	الحق	The Truth	*Al-Haqq*
52	الوكيل	The Trustee	*Al-Wakil*
53	القوى	The Possessor of All Strength	*Al-Qawiyy*
54	المتين	The Forceful One	*Al-Matin*
55	الولي	The Governor	*Al-Waliyy*
56	الحميد	The Praised One	*Al-Hamid*
57	المحصى	The Appraiser	*Al-Muhsi*
58	المبدئ	The Originator	*Al-Mubdi'*
59	المعيد	The Restorer	*Al-Mu'id*
60	المحيي	The Giver of Life	*Al-Muhyi*
61	المميت	The Taker of Life	*Al-Mumit*
62	الحي	The Ever Living One	*Al-Hayy*
63	القيوم	The Self-Existing One	*Al-Qayyum*
64	الواجد	The Finder	*Al-Wajid*
65	الماجد	The Glorious	*Al-Majid*
66	الواحد	The One, the All Inclusive, The Indivisible	*Al-Wahid*
67	الصمد	The Satisfier of All Needs	*As-Samad*
68	القادر	The All Powerful	*Al-Qadir*
69	المقتدر	The Creator of All Power	*Al-Muqtadir*
70	المقدم	The Expediter	*Al-Muqaddim*
71	المؤخر	The Delayer	*Al-Mu'akhkhir*

Al-Awwal	The First	الأول	72
Al-Akhir	The Last	الآخر	73
Az-Zahir	The Manifest One	الظاهر	74
Al-Batin	The Hidden One	الباطن	75
Al-Wali	The Protecting Friend	الوالي	76
Al-Muta'ali	The Supreme One	المتعال	77
Al-Barr	The Doer of Good	البر	78
At-Tawwab	The Acceptor of Repentance	التواب	79
Al-Muntaqim	The Avenger	المنتقم	80
Al-'Afuww	The Forgiver	العفو	81
Ar-Ra'uf	The Clement	الرؤوف	82
Malik-al-Mulk	The Owner of All	مالك الملك	83
Dhu-al-Jalal wa-al-Ikram	The Lord of Majesty and Bounty	ذو الجلال و الإكرام	84
Al-Muqsit	The Equitable One	المقسط	85
Al-Jami'	The Gatherer	الجامع	86
Al-Ghani	The Rich One	الغني	87
Al-Mughni	The Enricher	المغني	88
Al-Mani'	The Preventer of Harm	المانع	89
Ad-Darr	The Creator of The Harmful	الضار	90
An-Nafi'	The Creator of Good	النافع	91
An-Noor	The Light	النور	92
Al-Hadi	The Guide	الهادي	93
Al-Badi	The Originator	البديع	94
Al-Baqi	The Everlasting One	الباقي	95
Al-Warith	The Inheritor of All	الوارث	96
Ar-Rashid	The Righteous Teacher	الرشيد	97
As-Sabur	The Patient One	الصبور	98
Al-Ahad	*The One, The indivisible*	الاحد	99

2.UNDERSTANDING ISLAM

Yusuf Islam, also known by his former stage name Cat Stevens, a British singer and songwriter, once said:

“I was searching for God all my life, and as I moved from one spiritual teaching to another, I came to see them as circles, so I decided to look at what it was at the centre of each of these circles; I saw Christianity as a circle, and at the centre of it was Christ. I saw Judaism as a circle, and at the centre of it was the Jewish identity. I saw Buddhism as a circle, and at the centre of it was the Self and overcoming it. When I came to Islam, I saw it as a circle, but at its centre I found only God, and God was Whom I was looking for all my life.”

WHAT DOES ISLAM REALLY MEAN?

The word 'Islam' إسلام is derived from the Arabic root *salam* سلام, meaning 'peace'. Islam also means to surrender or submit, meaning to submit oneself to God and His commandments to reach peace. This doesn't mean that you have to blindly do everything without questioning it (this is what most media want you to think about Muslims). Islam is a religion of logic as well as spirituality. In fact, seeking knowledge is an important part of our faith and there are many narrations reiterating the lengths the Prophet Muhammad's companions went to in order to learn about their religion.

As one of the largest and the fastest growing religions in the world, it is often misinterpreted. With 1.6 billion Muslims hailing from all corners of the globe, it is understandable that culture, society and lack of education can often lead to a different practice of Islam than its original intention. You will learn to differentiate Islamic ways from cultures and customs – it is important to understand that Islam is a religion revealed for mankind irrespective of race and status. It is not only for the Arab world. In fact, Asians form one of the largest communities of Muslims. The Quran is also a revelation for the unseen, including the *jinn* (also known as 'genies').

God describes His creation on many occasions: "Indeed We have created man out of sounding clay, out of black mud moulded into shape, whereas the *jinn* We had created before him out of the fire of scorching winds";[1] and "the Angels were created from light".[2]

THE QURAN, OUR HOLY REVELATION

"This is the Book, there is no doubt about it, a guidance for the God-fearing". [3]

1. The Rocky Tract – *Surah Al Hijr* (15:26-27)

2. Hadith source: Saheeh Muslim

3. The Cow – *Surah Al Baqarah* (2:2)

The Quran is the name of Islam's sacred book, which has remained authentic and true to its original form since God revealed it. He named it 'Quran' قرآن as referred to 68 times in the revelations – a new word for Arabs at the time, which is derived from Arabic words for 'to collect' القرء (*al-Qar*) and 'to recite' قرأ (*Qara*).

The Quran as it is known today was revealed to the Prophet Muhammad in 610 AD through the archangel Gabriel (*Jibrail*) in Makkah, Saudi Arabia – the holiest city in Islam. According to the story in the Quran, Muhammad was meditating in the cave of Hira, where he would occasionally retreat, when Gabriel came to him and ordered him to read and recite (literally *Iqraa* إقرأ in Arabic, which is the root of the word Quran) the message of God. This first revelation can be found in the first five verses of the chapter named 'The Clot' (*Surah Al Alaq*):

"Recite in the name of your Lord who has created; Created man out of a clinging cell mass; Read – for your Lord is the most Bountiful One; Who has taught the use of the pen; taught man what he did not know."

I recall thinking about the era of darkness in Makkah when this took place, and the great lengths Muhammad went to before this revelation to seek peace and meditate in solitude. He would walk away from the hustle and bustle of the pilgrim city, busy with idol-worshippers coming to visit the Holy Kaaba. His ancestor, Prophet Abraham had originally built this 'House of God' with his son Ishmael (*Ismail* in Arabic).

Their descendants remained custodians of the Kaaba, but over time people deviated and turned it into a sanctuary to worship idols, rather than the 'One God'.

I had just changed jobs after a burn-out; I felt exhausted and hollow. There was no better city in the world than Makkah for me to reconnect with myself and God, meditate, and feel fully energised again. Spontaneously, my husband Abdellah and I booked a short trip during an upcoming holiday. I had been to Makkah before, but this particular time I was not able to complete all the rituals of the smaller pilgrimage *umrah*. I didn't let this upset me too much; it was such an honour to be in this Holy city that truly never sleeps. At any given time, millions of Muslims around the world pray toward this direction, while thousands circumambulate around the Kaaba and I was right in the centre of this magnetic energy. Abdellah thought it was a good opportunity to climb up the 'Mountain of Light' (*Jabal al-Noor*) where the Cave of Hira is located. The taxi ride took around 20 minutes and, together with my ten-month-old baby wrapped around me, we reached the top of the mountain in the heat after a tiring climb that took a full hour. My heart was beating fast, partly as the anticipation was building with every step and partly because I hadn't worked out for a long time!

It was pretty awe-inspiring. Here I was, walking in the footsteps of the Prophet's wife Khadijah (may Allah be pleased with her), who would sometimes climb up to meet her husband and bring him food, while being mindful not to disturb him during his time of reflection. In his retreats, he would contemplate and ponder on the creation of the universe.

I could hear a beautiful, soft-voiced recitation of the Quran. The sun was setting on a breath-taking view of Makkah and worshippers were gathering on the very peak of the mountain, shuffling up to fit late-comers within the small spot. To my surprise, it was a little Asian boy reciting the Quran and leading the prayer for a group of adults. This moment moved me as I felt proud to be a part of this community in which believers are truly equal and respected, regardless of age and colour.

I took a moment to 'be present' and soak up my surroundings. I realised how much effort and time it would have taken the Prophet to reach this place all by himself just to meditate – a true inspiration. I also imagined him rushing down the same mountain on 'The Night of Power' (known as *Laylat al-Qadr*) after his first overwhelming encounter with the Archangel Gabriel. He ran to his wife Khadijah, who comforted him, and he later said about her: "She believed in me when people rejected me; she accepted Islam when people rejected me; and she helped and comforted me when there was no one to lend me a helping hand".[1]

God had sent me exactly where I needed to be at that point in my life, with a profound need to meditate.

Prophet Muhammad was illiterate and the remainder of the Quran was revealed orally to him by the Archangel Gabriel in a series of recitations over the course of the next twenty-three years. The Holy Quran is not only considered sacred, but God has also blessed it when He revealed that He would protect it: "It is We Ourselves who have bestowed this reminder from on high, and it is We who shall preserve it intact."[2] From the earliest times, Muslims have deployed unprecedented efforts to keep memorisations, and the scriptures that entailed, authentic. These are continuously and meticulously checked for authenticity as centuries pass. The tradition of transmitting the verses orally has perpetuated to this day.

A LITTLE BIT OF VOCABULARY

The Holy Quran was revealed in the Arabic language and is still understood today in its original form. Anyone who speaks and learns classical Arabic can read and understand the Quran; it is not a lost language like Aramaic, Sanskrit, etc. As a result, you may have noticed that many books, websites and speakers mix a lot of Arabic terms into their

1. Narrated by Aisha
2. The Rocky Tract, *Surah Al-Hijr* (15:9)

sentences, which is confusing if you're not Muslim or don't speak the language. In this book, I make it a point to write in English and to mention the Arabic terms so you can familiarise yourself with them and learn them if you wish. They are also all referenced in the last section of the book, 'Terminology'.

God's intention is for believers to understand and memorise the Quran and to recite it to the next generations.

Picture this: if every single copy of the Quran in the world disappeared, it would still very much live because thousands and thousands of Muslims from all corners of the globe and of all ages remember the one and unique Arabic version in its entirety and will continue to pass on their knowledge to the next generations.

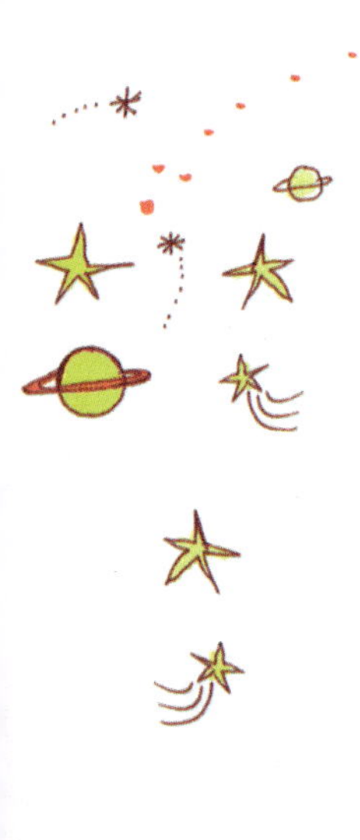

The Quran is made up of 114 chapters, each known as a *surah*. While the first verses to be revealed were mentioned earlier; the first chapter to be revealed in its entirety to the Prophet Muhammad is called *Surah Al Fatiha* and is important to know as we recite it in every prayer. It means 'The Opening' in English, as it is the Opening of the Book and of our prayers.

All chapters, with the exception of one, begin with the formula "In the Name of God, the Lord of Grace, the Ever-Merciful" – *Bismillah Ar-Rahman Ar-Rahim*. You will find it useful to learn this off by heart in Arabic, or just *Bismillah* (in the name of God), as we invoke God by His name whenever we are about to start something so that we can gain His blessing: before our first bite, when preparing a meal, starting the car, sitting an exam, etc.

The longest chapters are gathered in the beginning after *Al Fatiha* and gradually decrease in length. Therefore, the second chapter, 'The Cow' (*Surah Al Baqarah*), is the longest with 286 verses, while the shortest, made up of three verses is 'Abundance' (*Al Kawthar*) towards the end of the Quran.

To refer to a specific verse in the Quran, mention the number of the chapter and of the verse together. Each chapter is divided into numbered verses, called *ayat*. For example, 18:19 refers to the eighteenth chapter, 'The Cave' (*Al Kahf*), and its nineteenth verse, which marks the halfway point of the Holy book.

Chapters of the Quran are always referred to as a *surah* because, unlike a novel, they are not set in chronological order with an evolution of a story that has a beginning and an end. Verses were not chronologically revealed to Prophet Muhammad in the order they're arranged today. You can read it any way you prefer – personally, I enjoy reading it cover to cover, but every chapter can be read individually.

MIRACLES AND MYSTERIES OF THE HOLY QURAN: UNDERSTANDING AND RECITING

You may have heard people talking about the Quran as a miracle of God. It is described that way because of its linguistic brilliance and eloquence which no one – not even the biggest critics or literary geniuses – has been able to surpass or even imitate. For this reason, a verse of the Quran is called *aya* in Arabic, which means 'a sign' of God's miracles. It is also miraculous because of its content, which was far superior to the knowledge of that time. From physics and biology to cosmology and arithmetic, the advanced information hidden beneath rhetoric in the Quran is truly awe-inspiring. Another great miracle of the Quran is that the Arabic version remains the same as when it was first compiled, as mentioned earlier. There is no Quran 2.0 adapted for modern times – it is the word of God as it was originally intended and revealed.

The other monotheistic religions also had their respective miracles, such as Moses and Jesus and the miracles they performed in their respective eras. The Quran was revealed in Arabic, the language spoken by the Prophet Muhammad, but today it has been translated into most major African, Asian and European languages. The translation of the Quran is necessary, especially as most of the Muslims in the world are non-Arabic speakers.

However, translators admit that some of the original meanings and nuances of the Quran are lost in translation, and the original beauty and perfection of the Quran lies within the Arabic version. While this may be the case, it is important that non-Arabic speakers read the holy book in their own language first, to understand the message. One 'advanced' method of getting to know the Quran's meaning while appreciating its essence is to read it in both languages simultaneously – one paragraph in Arabic and then the translation. Islamic centres also hold *tafseer* classes (meaning 'interpretation') dedicated to this practice, and these are a good way to understand the depth of its verses and start learning classical Arabic.

Whatever language you read the Quran in, you may find that sometimes you don't understand the meaning of certain verses or chapters. To help you look beyond the initial layers and understand the deeper meaning, it's a good idea to take note of your questions and to ask around. Some translated copies of the Quran include notes on the historical and social context of verses at the time of their revelation – these are very helpful. Be wary of what you find on the internet – there's a lot of false information out there on Sheikh Google, so don't follow everything you read online blindly.

I recommend you to stick with a well-respected translator, such as Adil Salahi, whose English version '*The Qur'an: A Translation for the 21st Century*' I have used throughout this book. Women have also risen to the challenge, *Saheeh International* being a popular interpretation and the work of a lifetime for three American women who embraced Islam in the 1980s.

Hearing the call to prayer in a Muslim country is soul-soothing and hearing a recitation of the Quran can be mesmerising. As they strike a certain rhythm and melody, you may think the *muezzin* or reciter is singing. The practice of reciting with correct pronunciation is called *tajweed* and Islamic centres offer classes. When attending a *tajweed* class you will quickly realise that this skilful practice comes with its own rules. Recitations are a beautiful way to meditate and many contests are held across the world, for all ages. As Muslims we are strongly encouraged not only to learn the Quran but also to ponder its meaning. The more one reads and thinks about Allah's message, the more its depth and beauty reveals itself.

These classes are available for free in most Islamic centres to help you learn and remember verses for your prayers. Some of these centres even offer live classes online.

The shorter verses at the end of the Quran are the ones we first learn by heart. You will be surprised how quickly you will remember these! This practice is surprisingly rewarding as you will feel a huge sense of achievement when you memorise a chapter.

THE BEGINNINGS OF ISLAM, THE PROPHETS AND MESSENGERS

Muslims believe that Islam has existed since the birth of time but has only been known by the name 'Islam' since the Quran was revealed to the Prophet Muhammad. Given that Adam was the first Prophet, and also the first human to be created by God, it makes sense that Islam (as in 'to worship and surrender to God') came into existence at the same time. Muslims also believe that Adam, Moses, Jesus and other Messengers brought the 'Islam' of their respective eras – until those religions evolved to the extent that God's message became distorted and a new Prophet was chosen to reintroduce and to reestablish the truth. Therefore, Islam is a continuation of the monotheist religions including Judaism and Christianity.

A lot of non-Muslims are often surprised that Jesus and Moses are respected Prophets in Islam (known as *Issa* and *Musa* in Arabic). In fact, the Biblical Prophets are recognised

I become more than ever convinced that it was not the sword that won a place for Islam in those days. It was the rigid simplicity, the utter self-effacement of the Prophet, the scrupulous regard for pledges, his intense devotion to his friends and followers and his intrepidity, his fearlessness, his absolute trust in God and in his own mission. These and not the sword carried everything before them and surmounted every obstacle.

Gandhi

in Islam as well and twenty-five of them are mentioned in the Quran: Ishmael is known as *Ismail*, David as *Dawud*, Abraham is *Ibrahim*, Noah is *Nuh*, Jacob is *Yaqub*, Joseph is *Yusuf* and so on (peace be upon them). For Muslims, Muhammad is known as the 'Seal of the Prophets', as mentioned in verse 33:40:

"Muhammad is not the father of any one of your men, but is God's Messenger and the seal of all Prophets. God has indeed full knowledge of everything."

As Muslims, we always say, 'peace and blessings be upon him' (abbreviated as 'PBUH'); or in Arabic, *Sall Allahu Alay-hi wa-sallam* (sometimes abbreviated as SAW, or ﷺ in Arabic written form) when we talk about Prophet Muhammad, as instructed in the Quran: "God and His angels bless the Prophet. Believers! Bless him and give greetings of peace".[1] This might sound confusing at first when you hear people say, '*Muhammad Sall Allahu Alay-hi wa-sallam*' and you might think it is his full name. When you hear this, simply repeat the same formula after them.

Muslims also pay their respect to his wives and companions by saying, 'May Allah be pleased with her/him' – in Arabic, *radi Allah 'Anha* (for a female companion, or *'Anhu* for a male). For all Prophets and Messengers of God, as well as the Archangel Gabriel, we say, 'peace be upon him' (*Alayhi Salaam*).

Islam was undivided at the time the Quran was being revealed and the Muslim community was one. Nowadays, there are different divisions in Islam. Sunnis and Shiites developed into distinct communities because of their conflicting views about how religious authority was transmitted after the Prophet. Other than that, they practice Islam mostly in the same way.

1. The Combined Forces, *Surah Al-Ahzab*, (33:56)

It can be confusing, especially for someone new to Islam. The most important thing to remember is that all Muslims believe in the same fundamental acts of faith, and the differences only come into play over the details. Remember, Islam is a complete way of life known as the *deen* and its Prophet gave examples on how to live every aspect of it – from what to do when a baby is born to who should inherit at the time of death, and everything in between. It's no surprise that there are differences of opinion when it comes to some of the fine print!

The difference of opinion in varying details is partly due to the fact that the Prophet did some things in different ways, all of which are considered correct. Leaving room for interpretation was intentional, so as not to constrain us or to make things difficult for us.

TEACHINGS OF THE PROPHET: *HADITH* AND *SUNNAH*

As mentioned earlier, Islam is a complete way of life and, despite it being revealed over 1,400 years ago, Islam today remains very much true to its original message. This is due to several factors, including the fact that the Quran has been protected since it was first revealed, but also because God made the Prophet's life a practical example for us to follow.

Prophet Muhammad went through all the same motions of life that many of us can relate to: grief, persecution and exile, but also love, family, friendship and more. The Prophet's exemplary behaviour throughout these moments in his life are not mentioned in the Quran, but his actions (known as *sunnah* in Arabic) were recorded by his companions and passed down the generations in *hadiths* (sayings).

The Prophet Muhammad is the perfect role model for every Muslim, men and women alike. Everything he did – from the way he ate to the way he slept and the way he conducted business – he did for a beneficial reason, and while the Quran is a comprehensive guide for Muslims, the *hadith* and *sunnah* go into a lot more detail and shed light on the nitty gritty of everyday life. Together, the Quran and the *sunnah* are both essential to the understanding and practice of Islam.

Analysing the chain of narration of a *hadith* is a precise science, being classified as 'strong' (*sahih* in Arabic), 'good' or 'weak' according to the reliability of the narrator and the strength of the chain. Many elements are factored into the classifying process, including reviewing the history, reliability and authenticity of the narrator and every person in the chain of narration – from when the *hadith* was authenticated, traced back to the companion of the Prophet who narrated it – and evaluating the texts against the Quran to ensure there are no violations or contradictions.

There are six major *hadith* collections, among which 2,200 traditions have the highest status of authenticity, compiled in *Sahih Al-Bukhari* and *Sahih Muslim*. As a rule of thumb, remember that these authentic *hadith*s are usually labeled as *sahih* in Arabic, so you can easily recognise them. Other trusted sources from the main collections include *Sunan Abu Dawood, Jami al-Tirmidhi, Sunan al-Sughra, Sunan ibn Majah* and *Muawatta Malik*.

We must be careful, as people love to throw them around to make a point without referencing the source, sometimes without checking whether they are out of context or even made up entirely – their intention may be good, since Muslims are cautioned against quoting verses out of context, so supporting *hadiths* help. But certain *hadiths* have been classified as 'fabricated' and 'denounced'! When embracing Islam, we can feel a sense of restlessness to gather as much knowledge as quickly as possible and catch up. The fervency of a new Muslim is something I admire to this day! But an inquisitive mind is a positive trait and if something sounds off or illogical to you, you might need to go the extra mile and check the source – perhaps the translation they used was wrong? Maybe they have thrown their own culture into the mix? The companions of the Prophet would often ask for the source to ensure there were no falsifications and it is still common practice, so don't hesitate to dig a bit deeper.

You could use the search engine sunnah.com on your own, but don't be afraid to ask a trusted scholar or teacher for help – understanding the meaning of *hadith* can be complicated, and even an authentic *sahih hadith* can be misleading if you don't understand the context in which it was said.

Although it is unlikely you will check out the authenticity of every single *hadith*, you may find yourself in a particular situation where you're not sure what the Islamic ruling would be. Remember that the ruling may be unique to your particular circumstance, hence asking a trusted scholar would be more useful than online research. The corpus of Islamic scholarship is vast and there is no reason why you should not be able to find the right person to advise you. They will apply the historical context of the Quran and the *sunnah* in our time and place to offer advice based on the classical scholars' exegesis and interpretations.

If you're interested to study the science of *hadith*, many Islamic centres offer courses, starting with the forty *hadith* of Imam Nawawi, one of the most important compilations of narrations we have today.

THE DIFFERENT TYPES OF PEOPLE YOU WILL ENCOUNTER

Islam is a simple religion; its message is clear – but mankind just loves to complicate simple things. This is proven in many stories in the Quran, such as the stories of the cow during the time of Prophets Moses (2:67-71) and Salih with the she-camel (7:73-79). In fact, believing in one God, the Prophet Muhammad and all other Prophets makes you a Muslim already. Being a practising Muslim, however, is a different story. You will experience people judging you – maybe for your pre-Islamic life, maybe because of the way you choose to practise now or because you're from a different cultural background to theirs.

Grab your copy of the Quran to read the full stories.

God mentions these differences in the Quran, advising us to embrace our differences:

"Mankind! We have created you all out of a male and a female, and have made you into nations and tribes, so that you might come to know one another. Truly, the noblest of you in the sight of God is the one who is most genuinely God-fearing. God is all-knowing, all-aware."[1]

It only makes sense that every geography has their own cultural context. When I lived in Oman, I didn't immediately notice that there was a nuance between Arabic customs and Islamic traditions, and had mistakenly associated the two together!

As I got closer to the Muslim community, I realised it was made of different nationalities, races and personalities. I was able to differentiate the two and realised I could adapt my new Islamic way of life to my own background – I could stay true to my identity, my values and my education, as long as they did not contradict with the Quran and *sunnah*.

One of my African-American friends immediately spotted this contrast when embracing Islam in New York City and felt pressured to dress like the other men, speak Arabic and even quickly marry! He felt as though he was asked to change everything about himself to emulate their own cultural practices – this was more than what he signed up for!

1. Private Apartments, *Surah Al-Hujurat* (49:13)

Pushing a cultural directive under the imperative that it is an Islamic prescription is not acceptable and this can often introduce an added burden that creates hardships for new Muslims. As my friend visited other mosques, he met younger brothers that welcomed him with a different attitude. Sometimes you need to find the community that fits you best!

While he was going through this trial, we talked about what culture meant to us at great length. Islam does not eliminate culture. We decided to use our common sense and take into consideration the changes that were beneficial for ourselves and take the necessary steps to embrace what felt right naturally, in our own time. Some things that were asked of him were not required to be changed. We also recognised that in some communities, brothers and sisters of colour are less welcomed than I probably was, because I'm white. These are real issues that need to be addressed within the community.

It's easier said than done, but try not to let judgmental people bother you. Ultimately, what God thinks of you is what matters, and true friends will support you and encourage you regardless of any mistakes you make during your journey.

Try to remember that judgement is reserved for Allah alone and no one has the right to label one Muslim 'pious' or not over another. **Only God knows what is in people's** hearts beyond their appearances.

Due to the current political climate and acts of terrorism that are being committed in Islam's name, problematic terms are being used in the media, such as 'Islamists', where such acts of terror are not Islamic in any way. 'Extremist' or 'fundamentalist' are also relatively new terms created by non-Muslims to describe both Muslims who are 'extreme' in their beliefs and the way in which they try to impose their views on others. 'Islamic', another common term, may describe a Muslim who strives to practise Islam to the fullest but may not be politically driven.

You'll probably find that most Muslims are wary of labels and prefer not to be stereotyped or pigeon-holed, especially when it comes to something as personal as faith.

> "Never allow your hatred of any people to lead you away from justice. Be just, this is closer to righteousness.[1]"

Should you be afraid of *jihad*? What the word really means is an 'effort', of which two types are mentioned: the greater and lesser *jihad*. What the media uses *jihad* to refer to – fighting an oppressor – is actually the lesser (and outer) *jihad*. Battling one's personal spiritual struggles for virtue is the greater (and inner) *jihad*.

God advises us to repel evil with good and of course, killing is denounced in Islam, as clearly described in the following verses in the Quran:

1. The Table Spread, *Surah Al-Ma'idah* (5:8)

> Whoever kills a person it is as though he has killed all mankind. And whoever saves a life, it is as though he had saved all mankind.[1]

I highly recommend the book Muhammad: His Life based on the Earliest Sources, by Martin Lings

As mentioned earlier, it is important to analyse the historical context in which each verse of the Quran was revealed. Some were revealed to Prophet Muhammad after Muslims were chased out of town by his own tribe, hence his migration to the neighbouring city of Madinah (the second holiest site in Islam). If you're interested to know more, I highly encourage you to read books on the life of Prophet Muhammad.

In today's age where all eyes are on the Muslim community, showing the beauty of Islam through random acts of kindness is the best way to promote a message of peace and tolerance to the world. After all, actions speak louder than words! As a community, the Prophet commanded us to remove a wrong with a right in any situation, which is especially fitting to counter Islamophobia. Fear and hatred should not be answered with hatred and fear - it only creates more hatred in the world.

Interestingly, the founders of the different schools of thought in Islam strove to build a culture of tolerance, acceptance and intellectual growth within the Muslim community. They respected each other's opinions when differences arose. Likewise, we should behave respectfully towards our Muslim sisters and brothers of different backgrounds, even if their practices may vary somewhat.

1. The Table Spread, *Surah Al-Ma'idah* (5:32)

3. THE FIVE PILLARS OF ISLAM

The pillars of Islam ideally shape the practical aspect of our acts of worship – as we've all experienced, faith can fluctuate and this blueprint helps us stay connected to God and keep our faith alive in our hearts. They were made mandatory as a baseline which helps us evaluate our level of practice and areas of improvement. Like any foundation, the absence of one pillar can cause the others to become precarious or even fall down.

1. Testimony of Faith – *shahada*

As mentioned earlier, you're already a Muslim once you believe in one God and that Muhammad is His Messenger. It is not enough to keep it in your heart, though: the first step to 'officially' become Muslim with God as a witness is to pronounce the testimony of faith – known as the *shahada*.

"
لَا إِلٰهَ إِلَّا ٱللهُ مُحَمَّدٌ رَسُولُ ٱللهِ

lā ʾilāha ʾillā llāh muḥammadun rasūlu llāh

There is no god but God. Mohammad is the messenger of God.
"

This first pillar applies to 'born Muslims' also. If you embrace Islam, you can also add in this sentence that you believe that, as well as Muhammad, Jesus, Moses and Abraham were also His Messengers. You should not do this alone: a minimum of two Muslims should hear it as witnesses. The reason for this is that Islam emphasises the importance of being part of the community and this will help to introduce you to it. You can visit a mosque or an Islamic centre to do this, or ask your Muslim friends, colleagues or acquaintances to help you. One beautiful saying emphasising the way that God is waiting for us to come to Him is, "Take one step towards Me, I will take ten steps towards you. Walk towards me, I will run towards you!"[1]

2. Prayer

God prescribes prayer many times throughout the Quran as the most beneficial way for us to strengthen our faith and communicate with Him. I have dedicated a full chapter to prayer due to its importance in Islam, but in a nutshell, there are five daily prayers that each Muslim is obligated to perform, and a series of movements you have probably seen on TV. There are many ways for us to communicate and pray to God other than this one, though, such as holding one's hands out and speaking to Allah or remembering Him in our hearts.

1. Hadith Qudsi

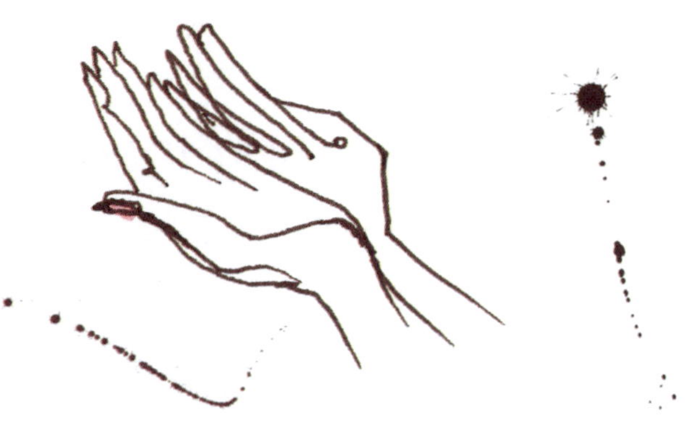

“It is indeed in the remembrance of God that people’s hearts find their comfort.[2]”

2. Thunder, *Surah Ar-Ra’ad* (13:28)

It's a really beautiful thing, knowing that at the same time, all across the world, Muslims come together, either in congregation or on their own, to connect and communicate with God. Watching hundreds or even thousands of Muslims praying together and moving in unison in a mosque can be a really powerful and even emotional experience. Non-Muslims who would like to observe the prayer can just contact the mosque first to arrange a visit.

3. Charity

Charity given to the poor and needy is obligatory in Islam for those with the financial means to do so. In Arabic, *zakah* (social welfare tax) literally means 'purification' because it's a way for us to purify our wealth and our heart. Each Muslim calculates the amount individually based on how much wealth they are in possession of and arranges to distribute a 2.5% share, either to poor people they know personally, through friends and relatives, or through Muslim charities. There is no need to be rich – every charitable act, big or small, goes a long way in Islam. In fact, even a smile is considered as a charitable act (*sadaqa*) – so imagine how much good you can bring to the world! As with every act of worship in Islam, our intention is the main thing. Everything we do, we do it to please God. Charity in particular should be done discreetly. After all, when no one knows that you've donated half your wages to a relief fund, you can be sure that your intention is pure! There's a famous saying highlighting this: "Charity should be so discreet that the left hand is unaware of what the right hand is giving."[1]

4. Fasting

Ramadan is the name of the ninth month in the Islamic lunar calendar. During this month, we fast from the first light of dawn until sunset, every day. But it's not only about

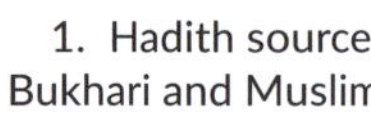

1. Hadith source: Bukhari and Muslim

abstaining from food and water. There are countless physical, spiritual and emotional benefits to fasting, including learning self-control, becoming closer to Allah, avoiding idleness, bad language or getting angry – and, of course, remembering the needy. Ramadan is the best opportunity to push a 'reset button' once a year, to look back on your progress and to strive to be a better person.

5. Pilgrimage to Makkah

Known as *hajj*, the major pilgrimage to the Holy Kaaba in Makkah is performed during the twelfth and final month of the lunar calendar. As Muslims, we are obligated to perform *hajj* once in our lifetime, provided we have the financial means to do so and are physically fit. It is an amazing and gruelling experience with rituals that date back to the time of the Prophet Abraham. It's the one time of the year when Muslims from all corners of the globe – from remote villages in Africa to skyscrapers in Singapore – come together for the exact same purpose, regardless of race, culture or social class. Not to be confused with *umrah*, the lesser pilgrimage, which is recommended but not compulsory and can be performed anytime.

One thing I found extremely beautiful when I first visited Makkah was just seeing Muslims from all corners of the globe dressed in their cultural attire and going through the same motions as each other. There were Africans in colourful cotton dresses, Malaysians in brilliant white headscarves and matching long skirts, Pakistanis in traditional baggy trousers and loose long tops, and Gulf Arabs in jet black abayas and scarves. Despite our cultural differences, we are all the same in the eyes of God and we were all there to worship Him in the same way.

THE SIX ARTICLES OF FAITH

While the five pillars form the foundation of our faith, the six articles are more about our beliefs than actual acts of worship. Every Muslim, in order to be so, should learn and think about these in depth.

Can you believe that the first ten years of revelations focused solely on building and strengthening these beliefs among the first Muslims? The details of living an Islamic life were only gradually revealed later, once the companions of the Prophet absorbed the truth of these articles of faith with utter conviction.

1 *Allah*, as the one and only God

The Angels 2

3 The Holy Books (this isn't just the Quran but also the original Gospel revealed to Jesus, the original Torah revealed to Moses and the Psalms revealed to David)

The Prophets. Islam counts a total of 124,000 prophets, out of which 313 are messengers. Twenty-five messengers are mentioned in the Quran, including Moses, Jesus, David, Abraham, Joseph, Jonah, etc. 4

5 The Day of Judgement – the day when every human will be judged for their deeds before entering Heaven or Hell

Predestination – believing that everything, good and bad, happens with God's will and knowledge but people still have freedom of choice and are responsible for their own actions 6

HALAL VS *HARAM*

Heard these terms before? I'm pretty sure you have seen *halal* signs in supermarkets and heard that something is '*haram'* as a figure of speech. The word has been distorted and is used in everyday language for something that is not good or should be avoided, not necessarily in the way that God intended to use it – which can lead to confusion!

When learning about Islam, the 'dos and don'ts' can often seem quite daunting – especially the 'don'ts'! When learning about what is permissible (*halal*) and what is not (*haram*) in the literal sense, remember that God uses these very sparingly and for very specific things. Besides, our Creator knows best what is good and bad for us.

When I became Muslim, I admit I was overwhelmed by the amount of people advising me not to wear this type of shirt, that I wasn't allowed to go to my favourite hang-out anymore or that Oreo's are *haram*… the list goes on! Luckily, my fervent enthusiasm didn't allow me to jump to conclusions – with research, I realised some of it was good advice, but not all. Islam is not a set of 'do's and don'ts' nor is it all black or white – there are degrees of permissibility in between.

It is important as a student of Islam to assemble a strong foundation of knowledge and understanding, built upon the articles of faith and the pillars of Islam, without which faith can easily be shaken. Just because a born-Muslim, someone who may have come to Islam before you or even a public speaker, says something is forbidden, doesn't mean they're right.

Keep in mind God is forgiving and merciful – so while we should strive to avoid impermissible acts, we shouldn't give up or lose hope if we find ourselves slipping once in a while. It is important to try our best and to strive for balance and progress, as faith is a journey and not a destination. God never tires of us asking for His forgiveness.

"[Thus speaks God]: You servants of Mine who have transgressed against their own souls! Do not despair of God's mercy: God forgives all sins; He alone is much-forgiving, ever- merciful."[1]

Did you know that the word '*haram*' has various meanings, depending on the pronunciation and Arabic spelling? It can mean 'forbidden' or 'impermissible,' but can also mean 'sanctuary' or 'sacred' such as *Masjid Al Haram*, which refers to the Sacred Mosque in which the Holy Kaaba is located.

1. The Troops, *Surah Az-Zumar (39:53)*

CHAPTER

A WAY OF LIFE

"Take benefit of five before five: your youth before your old age, your health before your sickness, your wealth before your poverty, your free time before you are preoccupied, and your life before your death".[1]

Prophet Mohammad

Well-being, self-care… these kinds of popular marketing terms are used in advertising campaigns to sell us products. They are not strange notions to us Muslims – we believe that our bodies belong to God and that they have been entrusted to us. If a friend gave you a car to look after for a few months, you wouldn't go and ramp up the mileage, drive recklessly, build up a collection of speeding tickets and intentionally get into accidents. Likewise, our bodies are vessels that will return to their Creator after our death. He has trusted us to look after it, not abuse it with nicotine, caffeine, fatty foods, a sedentary lifestyle.

This vessel will carry you through life, giving you a chance to laugh, a heart to love with and maybe the opportunity to have children.

1. Narrated by Ibn Abbas and reported by Al Hakim

It is our responsibility to look after this gift that has been given to us – and we have so much to gain from looking after our bodies. Do you want a body that allows you to enjoy life, to achieve your goals, to be there to look after your family for years to come? Because that power is in your hands.

"To some, Islam is nothing but a code of rule and regulations," says author and public speaker Yasmin Mogahed. "But, to those who understand, it is a perfect vision of life."

Truly every aspect of life is taken into consideration in Islam, which is why it is not just a religion but a holistic way of life – known as the *deen* in Arabic. The Quran is quite clearly split into two sections: the Makkan period and post-migration. The Makkan chapters (revealed before the Prophet migrated to Madinah) focus more on the fundamentals of Islam. The Madinan chapters (revealed after the Prophet's migration to Madinah) are more about social, community and everyday concerns – including respecting and taking care of our bodies, our heart and mental health.

Over time, adopting this lifestyle will allow spiritual growth and your serene energy will positively influence those around you.

Fasting and prayer are two pillars of Islam that focus not only on the spiritual rewards but on our bodies. Through this chapter, you will understand how these incredible self-care actions have personal benefits, as well as showing our respect for the human body and nature.

Let's connect our body, mind and soul – the Islamic way. Are you ready to reboot?

1. FASTING BENEFITS FOR THE BODY

"Believers, fasting is decreed for you as it was decreed for those before you, so that you may be God-fearing. Fast on a certain number of days. But whoever of you is ill, or on a journey, shall fast instead the same number of days later on. Those who find fasting a strain too hard to bear may compensate for it by feeding a needy person. He who does good of his own account does himself good thereby. For to fast is to do good to yourselves, if you only knew it.

"It was in the month of Ramadan that the Qur'an was revealed: a guidance for mankind and a self-evident proof of that guidance and a standard to distinguish right from wrong. Therefore, whoever of you is present in that month shall fast throughout the month; but he who is ill or on a journey shall fast instead the same number of days later on. God desires that you have ease. He does not desire that you be afflicted with hardship. You are, however, required to complete the necessary number of days and to extol and glorify God for having guided you aright and to tender your thanks.

"If My servants ask you about Me, well, I am near; I answer the prayer of the supplicant when he calls to Me. Let them then respond to Me, and believe in Me, so that they may follow the right way.

"It is lawful for you to be intimate with your wives during the night preceding the fast. They are as a garment for you, as you are for them. God is aware that you have been deceiving yourselves in this respect, and He has turned to you in His mercy and pardoned you. So, you may now lie with them and seek what God has ordained for you. Eat and drink until you can see the white streak of dawn against the blackness of the night. Then resume the fast till nightfall. Do not lie with your wives when you are in retreat in the mosques. These are the bounds set by God, so do not come near them. Thus God makes clear His revelations to people, that they may remain God-fearing."[1]

So, you already know that our fourth pillar in Islam, fasting, is not only about abstaining from food and drink from dawn to sunset. Throughout the whole month we should also strive to be a better person; to be more grateful and appreciative, more patient and polite; to give more to charity and try to help others, visit the sick and the elderly; and spend more time in worship. We also go the extra mile to abstain from lying, gossiping, swearing, cursing, backbiting and all other negative acts.

Fasting is also recommended outside of Ramadan as it holds many benefits – it is not only spiritually rewarding but it purifies our body, also. I've met many non-Muslims in the Middle East who are health-savvy and regularly fast the Islamic way for detoxing and well-being purposes, without the spiritual aspects. It was proven at the end of the nineteenth century that putting the digestive system to rest for a period of time holds great benefits.

When I was twelve years old and lived in the Sultanate of Oman, my best friend and I decided to try fasting for fun. I remember feeling really dizzy as we were ice-skating and I hadn't eaten since dinner the night before. Little did I know that I'd become Muslim and would master the art of fasting through trial and error over the years. The first year, I put on weight as I thought I should eat a big 'breakfast' to break my fast. So, I'd have melty chocolate cereals every evening and, needless to say, I piled on the pounds! Other years, I'd have headaches for the first few days, which I came to realise was a withdrawal symptom from not having an intake of caffeine,

1. The Cow, *Surah Al Baqarah* (2:183-187)

sugar and aspartame (what can I say, I was addicted to Diet Coke!). It made me stop drinking Diet Coke for good and I also learnt to gradually reduce my intake of caffeinated drinks at least ten days before Ramadan. My smoker friends similarly reduce their amount of nicotine.

Nowadays, my skin clears up during Ramadan; I have more energy and I'm more focused at work. I'm not saying it's all rosy and peachy – there are difficult moments – but I've realised that it's simply a matter of the body going through the different phases of the fasting process. Some days you will feel tired, but as your body becomes accustomed to it you will begin to thrive.

BREAKING FAST AROUND THE WORLD

I've said this before but I will never tire of saying it again and again: one of the most amazing things about Islam is that Muslims come from all corners of the globe, and while we all share our Islamic identity and culture, the way we practise it is enhanced by our diverse cultures.

When it comes to breaking fast (this is called *iftar* or *futoor* depending on the country) we all have our own little treats and foods that we associate with it. In the Middle East, most Muslims will start with dates, juice and then soup, followed by a main meal of meat/chicken and rice. In South East Asia, it's a time for fried samosas, pakoras, chickpeas and biryani. In North Africa, tagines are a must.

Wherever you are in the world, don't be afraid to create your own *iftar* meals that speak to you, that are adapted to your diet, your family and culture. But whatever you go for, try to keep it healthy, avoid fried snacks and, most importantly, don't overeat. It's supposed to be fasting, not feasting!

FASTING FOR HEALTH

Dr Henri Joyeux, a French cancer surgeon and author, published an article, 'Breaking Fast during Ramadan and Health', in which he described the most effective method to break fast and the health benefits of fasting. He also warned against over-eating, which is very common in many cultures. Here are a few of his tips:

1. Have a hearty and healthy breakfast before dawn. This meal is called *suhoor* – prepare it the night before if you can. Enjoy seasonal fruits for their minerals, vitamins and fructose (the best form of sugar) and eggs for a healthy amount of cholesterol.

2. Break your fast with one to three dates, as Prophet Muhammad did, and a colourful salad and soup.

3. Avoid hyper-caloric dinners when breaking your fast – over-nutrition is responsible for many illnesses which target all organs: thyroid, skin, digestive and nervous systems, and different forms of cancer. So, avoid fried and rich foods – the extra calories will transform into fat stored in the liver, which causes chronic fatigue and can result in further consequences.

4. Be careful not to consume sugars in excess, which can become addictive (canned juices, yoghurts).

5 Animal protein can overload the digestive system and mess up your sleep. And trust me, you'll need quality sleep!

6 Ideally, remember the 80/20 rule throughout the year: consume 80% vegetables and 20% animal products.

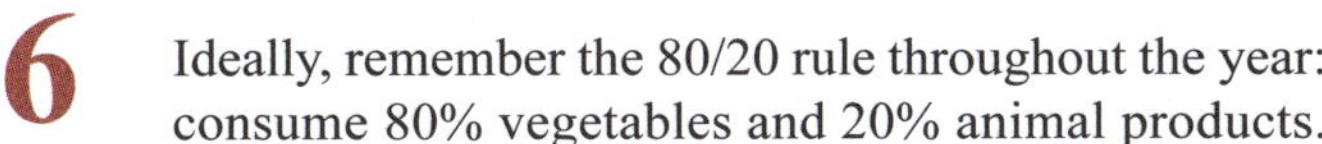

7 It is essential to hydrate yourself by drinking continuously from sunset through to dawn, especially in the hot and long summer days, to avoid dehydration. Aim for a minimum two litres of water – think soups for iftar, herbal tisanes, coconut water, smoothies, fruits and vegetables, etc.

He concludes by saying: "The Holy month of Ramadan can be a suitable time to reflect on the strong connection between food and health. It is a month in which one should lose weight (more body fat than muscle mass), where fasting reduces arterial hypertension and arthritis pain, relieves psoriasis, and the liver can get rid of fat."

A lot of non-Muslims wish me good luck at the start of Ramadan, or try to comfort me by saying that it will pass quickly. They have it all wrong. We Muslims absolutely love the Holy month – we're excited when it begins and sad when it ends. It is like inviting a dear old friend to your home for a month: you'll be psyched to see her, will cherish your days in her presence, and will be tearful to see her leave for a year.

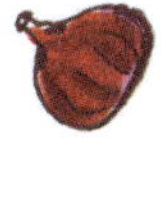

FASTING OUTSIDE OF RAMADAN

We don't just fast during the Holy month. Sometimes we fast in other months to make up for the days we might have missed during Ramadan – if we were sick, travelling, pregnant, breastfeeding or on our period. Sometimes we fast during other Holy times of the year as well, like the month of *Muharram*. Other times we fast to follow the tradition of Prophet Muhammad by fasting on a Monday and/or Thursday.

There are loads of benefits to regular fasting, both spiritual and physical. Spiritually it strengthens our connection with God and adds to our account of good deeds. Physically, it keeps us healthy.

One more benefit of Ramadan is that it makes us appreciate the blessing of food and connect with the poor who don't have the luxury of food that many of us have.

But there's also another benefit to fasting. Ever heard of men being told to take a cold shower if they're turned on? Well, fasting works in the same way – for men and women. The state of fasting itself can make you calm and serene and less inclined to flirt or have sexual urges. So, if you're single and ready to mingle, you might want to try fasting on a regular basis while you find someone worthy of being your husband!

"Whoever among you possesses the physical and financial resources to marry should do so, because it helps one to guard their modesty, and whoever is unable to marry should fast, as fasting diminishes one's sexual desire."[1]

1. Hadith source: Saheeh Muslim

10 THINGS WOMEN NEED TO KNOW ABOUT FASTING

Over the years, I've learnt that fasting adjusts to personal circumstances. It is advisable to evaluate your health and speak to your doctor for a safe fast. A few pointers to consider and to help you get started in your research are:

1 Muslim women are exempt from fasting during their period as it is a time for our body to rest and detox. You can make up for missed fasts any time of the year, apart from the two *Eid* celebrations, and it's better to try and get them done before the next Ramadan, otherwise you might find yourself accumulating too many to make up!

Pregnant and breastfeeding women aren't required to fast either. Some women do 2
– maybe because they're in a country where the fasting hours are short and they don't want to make them up later. But listen to your body. God has given you a Get-Out-of-Fasting-Free Card so don't be afraid to use it! You can look into the options of how to make up for fasts missed during pregnancy and breastfeeding later.

3 Women who are still experiencing post-partum bleeding forty days after delivering are exempt from fasting, too.

You don't have to fast if you're sick or travelling more than forty-eight miles 4
either – again, you can make it up another time.

5 If you have a chronic health condition that stops you from fasting full-stop, or you are too elderly to fast, all you have to do is feed a fasting person for every fast that you miss. There is a set rate that you can pay depending on where you are in the world. Most international charities accept these donations, which makes it easier for you to manage.

Sexual intercourse with your husband during fasting hours nullifies the fast. 6

7 Deliberately throwing up invalidates the fast.

Eating or drinking accidentally does not break your fast – so just carry on fasting 8
but try to be more careful!

9 Smoking invalidates the fast.

You can brush your teeth and gargle so long as you don't swallow the water, but 10
miswak is preferable (keep reading to find out what it is!)

2. NATURAL MEDICINE

Looking after our bodies and adopting preventive methods to avoid illnesses goes hand in hand. In my family, we are big fans of essential oils therapy and my mother-in-law uses oils to make natural soaps, deodorants, preventive elixirs against the flu and what not.

I also happen to be a picky eater with a sensitive palate and became a vegetarian at an early age – nothing to do with ethical convictions, but just a matter of taste. Being a vegetarian is a personal choice and eating meat is absolutely fine in Islam; we'll go over the meaning of *halal* products and, more importantly, animal rights shortly.

Over the years I've also tried to learn natural ways to boost my metabolism and energy through power foods and natural medicine used by Prophet Muhammad. A hadith says, "Allah has not sent down a disease except that He has also sent down its cure."[1]

This chapter would not be whole without a brief introduction to the Golden Age of Muslim civilisation and its numerous advances made in biology, chemistry, physics and healthcare between the eighth and thirteenth centuries.

Floral water, also known as hydrolate, is one of many discoveries. We owe our precious rose water to the art of distillation, a process invented by the renowned alchemist Jabir ibn Hayyan, aka the 'Father of Arab chemistry', in the eighth century. Discoveries made during this time by Muslims include mercuric chloride to disinfect wounds, the technique of inoculation through vaccination, frequency analysis in cryptology and the windmill, to name a few.

1. Hadith source: Bukhari and Muslim

Numerous medical writings were left behind that have contributed to today's modern medical practice.

CUPPING

Cupping, or *hijama*, is an ancient health tradition in Chinese medicine also practised back in the days of the Prophet. It involves placing glass cups on certain areas of the body and then making small incisions in the flesh to draw out toxins. Its benefits include:

- boosting the circulatory and immune systems
- cleansing and detoxifying the body
- pain relief
- helping with fertility issues
- treating various muscular, skeletal, neurological, immune, cardio-vascular, respiratory, digestive and urinary issues.

The difference between the Islamic and traditional methods of cupping is that *hijama* is performed on specific spots on the body as instructed by the Prophet Muhammad (primarily on the upper back, which targets the heart, lungs, brain and spine) and during certain lunar days. The practitioner will also recite the Quran whilst performing the treatment.

If it's the first time you've heard of this treatment, you might think it's pretty bizarre. Glass cups? Cuts? To be honest, the temporary marks certainly do look as though you have been kidnapped by aliens and experimented on. Rest assured, it is a tradition practised in many countries, including Finland, Russia and, of course, the Islamic countries. In fact, it was discovered in China more than 5,000 years ago. It doesn't really hurt, either, and the scars heal quickly.

RUQYAH, OR THE POWER OF WORDS

No, *Ruqyah* wasn't one of the Prophet's daughters – that's Ruqayyah! *Ruqyah* is another natural healing method where various invocations from the Quran and other prayers are recited to heal and protect from illnesses, diseases and the evil eye. Sorry ladies, this term is not easy to translate into English so I'll leave it in its Arabic form!

Hamza Yusuf, an American revert and Islamic scholar once said: "Don't ever diminish the power of words. Words move hearts and hearts move limbs." I couldn't agree more; words can hurt, but they have the power to heal, too – especially if they are Divine. If talking to plants helps them grow, why not speak to our body? In Islam, we believe that it is God who heals – and everything heals through His will and power.

There are a few important things to note when it comes to performing *ruqyah*:

- The prayers must be either from the Quran or invocations taken from narrations of the Prophet, calling Allah to help.
- The intention must be made to Allah, and not to seek help from the formula of words itself – *ruqyah* is not a magic spell!
- Anybody can do it – but it cannot be performed by a magician or a soothsayer.
- All the words must be clearly understood.

10 BLESSINGS OF SURPRISING FOODS

Did you know that there are certain fruits and vegetables that are so rife with nutrition and health benefits that they are actually mentioned in the Quran and recorded in the narrations of many prophets?

God says in the Quran: "It is He who sends down water from the skies. From it you drink, and with it grow the plants on which you pasture your cattle. And with it He causes crops to grow for you, and olive trees, and date-palms, and grapes, and all other kinds of fruit. Surely in this there is a sign for people who think."[1]

1. Shine with Honey:

"Your Lord has inspired the bee: 'Take up homes in the mountains, in the trees and in structures people may put up. Then eat of all manner of fruit, and follow humbly the paths your Lord has made smooth for you'. There issues from its inside a drink of different colours, a cure for people. Surely in this there is a sign for people who think."[2]

This excerpt, taken from the chapter in the Quran called 'The Bee', reveals how honey is made and that the worker bee is female – which was only discovered by western science at the end of the sixteenth century!

Honey has been considered as medicinal gold for centuries for its antiseptic and antibiotic properties. Other ways honey can be used for a glowing skin include:

- Treating acne – honey is naturally antibacterial, so it's great for acne treatment and prevention.
- Anti-ageing – full of anti-oxidants, it's great for slowing down ageing.

1. The Bee, *Surah An-Nahl* (16:10-11)

2. The Bee, *Surah An-Nahl* (16:68-69)

- Boosting complexion – it's extremely moisturising and soothing, so it helps create a glow.
- Reducing pores – honey is clarifying because it opens up pores, making them easy to unclog.

2. Glow with Olive Oil and Olives

The olive tree and the fruit it bears both have a sacred importance in countless religions and are mentioned in the Bible and the Torah as well as the Quran.

In fact, in the Quran God describes Himself in the following manner:

God is the Light of the heavens and the earth. His Light may be compared to a niche containing a lamp; the lamp within a glass, the glass like a radiant star; lit from a blessed tree – an olive tree that is neither of the east nor the west. Its very oil would almost give light even though no fire had touched it. Light upon Light! God guides to His light him that wills [to be guided]. God propounds parables for all people, since God alone has full knowledge of all things.[1] ”

Just one of the sayings of Prophet Muhammad is, "Eat olive oil and apply it (topically), since there is cure for seventy diseases in it, [and] one of them is leprosy."[2]

1. The Light, *Surah An-Noor* (24:35)

2. Source: Abu Naim and Abu Aseed, Reported by al-Tirmidhi

HONEY
ROSE WATER
GRASS FED BUTTER
GOAT MILK
HONEY
HONEY
SHEEP MILK
HONEY

Some of its countless uses include:

- Ingesting it to regulate the digestive process.
- Using it as a tonic for gorgeous locks – it makes hair healthy and strong, as well as adding lustre.
- Massaging olive oil with ordinary salt over the gums is a remedy for several diseases of the gums and teeth.
- Applying it topically to heal chronic ulcers and boils, which are often difficult to heal.
- Combining normal saline and olive oil to treat burns.
- Soaking olive leaves in water is effective against mouth and lip ulcers, and dermatitis due to allergies.
- Bring the spa home! Massaging olive oil all over the body tones up the muscles and organs, and relieves muscular pain.

3. The Cure: Figs

You know a fruit is special when there's a whole chapter dedicated to it in the Quran – God swears "by the fig and the olive" in the chapter titled 'The Fig'.[1] In fact, the fig tree is one of five fruits mentioned in the Quran, along with olives, grapes, pomegranate and dates.

Figs have many health benefits. According to Abu Darda, one of the Prophet's companions, someone once presented figs to the Prophet Muhammad, who distributed them among his companions, saying, "Eat it as it cures various diseases".

Fresh and dry figs are high in pectin, a soluble fibre that can reduce blood cholesterol. The fruit also has a laxative effect and can aid those who suffer from chronic constipation.

In Islam, figs are a fruit from Paradise. They are a rich source of calcium, iron, magnesium, vitamin B6, and potassium. They're low in fat and provide more fibre than any other common fruit or vegetable.

1. *Surah Al Teen*

4. Refuel with Dates

Dates have become synonymous with Islam mainly because they are consumed a lot during the Holy month of Ramadan, as Prophet Muhammad used to break his fast with them. There's also a beneficial reason behind the tradition.

To begin with, they are rich in several vitamins, minerals and fibre and they contain oil, calcium, sulphur, iron, potassium, phosphorous, manganese, copper and magnesium, which are all hugely beneficial for our health. Just some of the health benefits of the super fruit include relieving constipation, intestinal disorders, heart problems, anaemia, diarrhoea, abdominal cancer, sexual dysfunction and many other conditions.

While there are hundreds of varieties, the most sought-after kind of dates for Muslims are called Ajwa – they come from Saudi Arabia, and more precisely from Madinah. It is said that the Prophet Muhammad freed a slave, Salman the Persian, whose master demanded forty ounces of gold and 300 date palms in exchange. The Prophet's companions contributed palm-shoots and helped Salman as he dug the holes to plant them. The Prophet said, "Mine is the hand that shall put them in" in order to bless the date trees. The plantations grew in record time, are thriving to date and Salman became a close companion of the Prophet.

Dates aren't just great in Ramadan, though. My sister-in-law prepared energy balls made from dates when I gave birth to my daughter, as it is recommended to eat dates during childbirth for a much-needed boost of energy. It is also a great food to eat if you're breastfeeding because it helps boost your milk supply.

5. Detox with Grapes

Allah mentions grapes in the Quran as a fruit of the people of Paradise: "And by means of this water We bring forth for you gardens of date-palms and vines, yielding abundant fruit, and from which you eat".[1]

The Prophet was very fond of grapes and there are numerous medicinal benefits to eating them, including purifying the blood, providing vigour and health, strengthening the kidneys and clearing the bowels.

6. The Anti-oxidant: Pomegranate

God says in the Quran, "It is He who has brought into being gardens – both of the cultivated type and those growing wild – and the date palm, and fields bearing different produce, and the olive tree, and the pomegranates, all resembling one another and yet so different. Eat of their fruit when they come to fruition, and give [to the poor] what is due to them on harvest day. But do not waste, for He does not love the wasteful."[2]

Pomegranates are another superfruit mentioned in the Quran. The most powerful anti-oxidant of all fruits, they also have tonnes of other health benefits, including:

- potent anti-cancer and immune supporting effects
- inhibit abnormal platelet aggregation that could cause heart attacks, strokes and embolic disease
- lower cholesterol and other cardiac risk factors
- lower blood pressure
- promote reversal of atherosclerotic plaque
- may have benefits to relieve or protect against depression and osteoporosis.

And here's something for all you curly haired girls: to get your locks under control, try a pomegranate seed oil treatment. Apply slightly warmed up oil to your hair and leave on for about an hour before washing; it will tame the frizz and moisturise your hair.

1. The Believers, *Surah Al-Mu'minun* (23:19)

2. The Cattle, *Surah Al-An'am* (6:141)

7. When Life Gives You Melons

The combination of the honeydew melon's high-water content and potassium levels is effective at maintaining healthy blood pressure levels. As honeydew contains both vitamin C and copper, it promotes healthy skin by aiding collagen production and tissue repair.

8. The Sunlight Vitamin: Mushrooms

Mushrooms and truffles are from the same family and have many of the same benefits. They are an important dietary source of essential amino acids. They are an excellent source of fibre, vitamins and some minerals like selenium. They are low in fat and free of cholesterol.

Mushrooms are the only vegetable and the second known source (after cod liver oil) to contain vitamin D, known as the sunlight vitamin, in edible form.

They are rich in calcium (good for bones), iron (benefits for anaemia), potassium (very good for lowering blood pressure), copper (anti-bacterial) and selenium (very good for bones, teeth, nails, hair and as an anti-oxidant).

The Prophet Muhammad said: "The truffle is among Allah's favours and its water cures the eye."[1] There's a reason why truffles are so expensive!

9. Barley Soup for the Soul

Heard of chicken soup for the soul? I bet you didn't know that the soothing benefits of soup were even relied on during the time of the Prophets!

Prophet Muhammad recommended that barley soup be made for the sick and those who were mourning a death. His wife

1. Hadith source: Bukhari and Muslim

Aisha narrated: "I heard the Messenger of God say that it soothes the heart of the sick and takes away some of the grief."[1]

10. The Surprising Cure: Vinegar

According to Aisha, the Prophet said, "The best of condiments is vinegar."[2] This isn't surprising given vinegar's numerous health benefits, including relieving:

- arthritic pains
- blood pressure
- uneven skin pigmentation
- bleeding gums
- high cholesterol
- yeast infections
- fungal infections

Today, apple cider vinegar has become a health food go-to for aiding weight loss, reducing blood sugar levels, curbing one's appetite and more. Don't be fooled by the word 'cider' – this vinegar is permissible, or *halal*, so you can gulp away! The best way to take it is by adding two tablespoons to a glass of warm water. You can add some raw, organic honey to it as well.

1. Narrated by Al-Bukhari and Muslim
2. Hadith Source: Muslim

3. PRAYING: A PHYSIO-SPIRITUAL PRACTICE

Prayer doesn't only contribute to a healthy mind through connecting with God; the actual movements positively benefit our mind and body as well. There are the obvious benefits like improving concentration and, from a physical perspective, stretching muscles and improving flexibility. But there's more to it than that.

Standing

Known to improve posture, balance and self-awareness, standing also regulates blood pressure and breathing.

The placement of the hands below the chest is said to activate the nerve pathway, which affects the health of the muscular system, skin, intestines, liver, pancreas, gallbladder and eyes. It also governs the health of the heart, lungs, thymus, immune system, and circulatory system.

Bending down

It stretches the muscles of the lower back, thighs, legs and calves, and allows blood to be pumped down into the upper torso. It tones the muscles of the stomach, abdomen, and kidneys. Forming a right angle allows the stomach muscles to develop, and can help prevent flabbiness in the mid-section.

Prostration

This nerve pathway relates to the health of the brain, nervous system, and pineal gland. The bending movement also promotes the health of the lymph and skeletal systems, the prostate, bladder, and the adrenal glands.

Sitting

This firms the knees, thighs and legs. It is said to be good for those prone to excessive sleep, and those who like to keep long hours. Furthermore, this position assists in speedy digestion, aids the detoxification of the liver and stimulates peristaltic action in the large intestine.

At the end, turning the head towards first the right and then the left shoulder in the closing of the prayer helps to relax the throat, neck and shoulders.

STAYING FIT FOR HAPPY VIBES

Fitness and being healthy is an integral part of being a Muslim. The Prophet Muhammad said in a narration that a strong believer is better than a weak believer.[1] According to the explanations of this narration, he wasn't just talking about faith but about character and physical strength as well. Being fit helps prevent disease and boosts our mood as well as our energy levels. Laziness and idleness are big no-nos in Islam and so is overeating. The Prophet was said to only eat until a third of his belly was full, and would fill one third with liquids and leave one third for air.[2]

Ibtihaj Muhammad, an American sabre fencer and modest-wear designer, is also known as the first Muslim American woman to wear a hijab while competing for the United States in the Olympics. She said, "I believe in the power of sports

1. Narrated by Abu Huraira
2. Source: Sunan ibn Majah

to bring people together across barriers of all kinds… and despite my wearing hijab, and being different, I was able to overcome the odds and succeed in sport".

Are you a yogi? Body positions in Muslim prayer may remind you of certain yoga postures.

You might be wondering; can you still practice yoga if you're Muslim? That's a million-dollar question amongst scholars and a heated one, too. First of all, what is your intention? While millions of Muslim women do yoga as a physical exercise nowadays, scholars warn against its religious origin and the act of worshipping other than God without realising it – for example, the 'salute to the sun' position and saying '*namaste*' (meaning 'I bow to the divine in you') when Muslims only bow before the one God.

Of course, yoga is a broader term in the West, and the practice has evolved to a form of physical exercise and restorative practice, unlike in the Hindu tradition.

So, to yoga or not yoga? In Islam, our actions depend on the intention behind them. As Muslims, everything we do should be done for God. If we exercise with the intention of keeping our bodies healthy in order to better serve God, then our intention – and the exercise – is in accord with Islam. So, when it comes to yoga, if you're just working out to stay fit and healthy and you don't chant anything related to the religious aspects of it, my understanding is that most say it is fine. Feel free to discuss this further with a scholar to feel comfortable with your own decision!

4.BEAUTY SECRETS

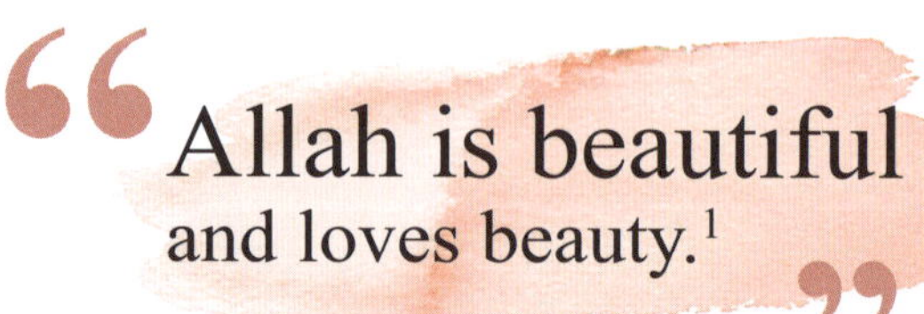

God is beautiful and His appreciation of beauty is manifested in His creation. There is beauty in everything, from a butterfly's delicate wings to vibrant green grass swaying in the breeze and, of course, the miracle that is the human body.

While physical beauty has no bearing on a person's status in Islam, Islam does recognise the role it plays. Do not let the illusion of beauty in the world of fashion and pop culture contradict your principles and values of modesty and humility. It is said that God's spiritual light, known as His *noor* as described earlier in this chapter, shows on a believer's face as a reflection of her soul. So, work on your heart for the perfect glow to illuminate your eyes and brighten your complexion!

Abusing our bodies with harmful substances and causing it harm is not reasonable as they have been entrusted to us and will one day return to God.

HAIR REMOVAL & HAIR CUTS

Whether you want to remove or keep hairs on your body is up to you, including whatever removal method you might choose (whether it is waxing, threading or shaving). There is a general consensus that the only recommended area to leave untouched is our eyebrows. We are told to leave our eyebrows be and, in my opinion, to only tidy them up slightly if they are completely unruly and masculine. Even then, though,

1. Hadith source: Muslim

we can only 'tidy' them and not shape them. The reason for this is that we're not supposed to permanently alter the way we have been created. This can be quite challenging, but one way of dealing with bushy eyebrows is bleaching the excess hair so it becomes almost invisible!

As for haircuts, there's nothing wrong with cutting your hair and we, as women, are encouraged to beautify ourselves so long as it is not for the eyes of any non-related men. However, shaving our hair completely isn't allowed unless for medical reasons – and, while we're on the matter, cross-dressing isn't acceptable either from my understanding. Women are encouraged to look like women and, likewise, men are encouraged to look like men.

Many aspects of a Muslim woman's way of life need to be considered by oneself, first, and any questions followed up with the support and knowledge of someone you trust. It is important to remember that it is what is in our hearts that matters much more than what we wear, and that ultimately, God is Merciful and wants us to be at peace within our bodies, minds, and souls.

MAKE-UP, TATTOOS AND BLING

Hair aside, what about make-up and tattoos?

The vast majority seems to agree that the former is absolutely fine so long as the products don't contain any harmful ingredients, it looks elegant and your phone's Face ID still recognizes you! The latter, according to my research at least, is largely frowned upon: tattoos, because of their permanent nature are seen as disfiguring and distorting God's creation. Tattooed eyebrows, or microblading, is included in this list! This seems to be the case for body piercings, too. Make-up you can just wipe off but tattoos and piercings are there to stay. If you already have one or several, you can seek advice from a scholar on what to do as there are different schools of thought.

When it comes to jewellery, women in Islam can wear precious stones and metals like gold and silver; including pierced earrings, since they were worn during the time of the Prophet, and nose rings (these are a part of many women's cultural heritage). So, bring on the sparkles but keep it modest, elegant and stay humble always.

NAIL AND BODY ART

If you like to paint your nails, it's worth knowing how and when to wear nail varnish, as opinions widely differ.

The issue with nail varnish is that it is not permeable – so when you perform your ablutions before prayer, water doesn't get to reach your actual nails, meaning your ablution isn't valid.

But what about all the Muslim women you've seen out and about with coloured nails? Well, it could be that they're on their period so they won't engage in prayer for several days.

There have been a few brands claiming their nail varnishes are water permeable, hence *halal*. My advice would be to do proper research into them, ask a scholar and then decide whether or not to wear it. To go natural, you can just buff your nails and apply some solar oil to get a shiny coat without any polish or opt to stain your nails with henna instead. It's a natural orange/brown dye which is applied directly on the skin and nails, and gradually fades after a few days. You've probably seen beautiful brides with henna drawn up from the tip of their fingers to their elbows and their ankles: it's real body art! However, stay away from the black kind as it contains a toxic chemical.

FEMININE HYGIENE AND BODY RULES

There is a great emphasis on cleanliness and hygiene in Islam. Like everything else in our religion, there are very clear and simple guidelines on how we can keep clean and what we need to do.

Intimate grooming

Keeping our underarms and private areas clean and hair-free is a must – for both men and women.

We should also wash 'down under' whenever we go to the toilet. In the Middle East or in Muslim countries, this is easy to do as all toilets are conveniently fitted with a water pipe so we can easily wash up. However, in non-Muslim countries it gets trickier. You can purchase bottles or little watering cans and keep them by the toilet to fill with water and then use for a quick rinse.

Our prayers aren't accepted if we are unclean so it is really important to take extra care washing those areas when we've been to the toilet. You can find out more about cleanliness and all types of ablutions in the 'Prayer' chapter.

In a nutshell, there are minor and major ablutions, which we also call mandatory baths. There are two instances when we must perform major ablutions: after our period and after sexual intercourse with our husband. During these baths, we have to wash our whole body (hair included) so that every centimetre of skin and hair is wet. We also have to gargle and rinse the insides of our nose in order to fulfil the requirements of the *ghusl*, or mandatory bath.

Oral hygiene

You might find this surprising, but Islam even mentions bad breath and oral hygiene. The Prophet used a *siwaak*, also known as *miswak*, which is essentially a twig with a frayed end that he used to clean his teeth throughout the day, even when fasting: "Were it not for the fact that I did not want to make things too hard for my *ummah*, I would have commanded them to use the *siwaak* at every time of prayer."[1]

SEXUALITY AND FAMILY PLANNING

Sex is not taboo in Islam, nor forbidden, wrong or filthy. In fact, contrary to public opinion, sex plays an integral role in Muslim married life and is supposed to be a pleasurable experience for women, too – so long as it is within the sanctity of marriage, of course.

Unfortunately, some cultures still mix their ultra-conservative views and their ancestors' traditions with our religion. The Prophet Muhammad himself used to give advice to his companions on how to conduct themselves with their wives and husbands for a respectful and healthy sexual life. However, one's sexual life should stay a private matter between husband and wife and should not be made public. What happens in bed stays in bed. I'll go into more detail about love and marriage in the 'Togetherness' chapter.

As with everything else in Islam, we are encouraged to educate ourselves on sexual matters and family planning.

There is a slight difference of opinion when it comes to contraception, with some scholars believing it not to be allowed in Islam. Today, however, many of the scholars agree that contraception is permissible. However, birth control pills are still a matter of controversy, not only in the

1. Narrated by Abu Hurairah

Muslim community, because of the effect and imbalances they cause within a woman's body. If you're like me and you prefer to keep things as natural as possible, there are natural contraception methods you can explore. I highly recommend *Taking Charge of my Fertility* by Toni Weschler if you're interested in learning about the subject.

So, what happens if you don't use contraception and you fall pregnant but you don't want to keep the baby?

Naturally, abortion is a sensitive topic for any parent and needs to be discussed with a doctor in the light of an individual's own circumstances. My observations conclude that, in Islam, most scholars believe that an abortion is only acceptable if the baby is less than 120 days old, which is approximately when a soul is blown into the foetus; and that it is only permissible for a significant reason. If the gynecologist diagnoses that the foetus is causing so much harm to the mother that giving birth endangers her life, the Islamic view point would be to save the mother's life by terminating the pregnancy.

Right, so you're having a baby? Congratulations! Let's talk about circumcision for a minute and specifically the elephant in the room. Whatever you've heard about female genital mutilation being an Islamic custom is completely and utterly wrong. There is no place for such customs in Islam and those who practise it do so because of their culture and traditions.

In Islam, circumcision is required for boys only and has nothing to do with reducing pleasure. Circumcision is for cleanliness reasons only, to prevent dirt from getting trapped in the foreskin and causing various infections. It is advised for boys to be circumcised as young as possible to avoid pain and discomfort – it's a basic procedure in hospitals nowadays.

5. ANIMAL WELFARE

In Islam, every living creature, from humans to animals and even plants, has rights. As the superior species, it is our responsibility to look after animals and take care of them with kindness, respect and mercy. Killing an animal as small as an insect or even inflicting mental cruelty are completely forbidden in Islam. It therefore goes without saying that hunting for sport is out of the question. We are only allowed to kill animals for food, and even then, there is a strict set of rules to follow in order to show respect.

In fact, there is an entire chapter of the Quran named 'The Ant', which tells us about an encounter between the Prophet Solomon – who had been given the very special gift of understanding and communicating freely with God's creatures – and a group of ants, as described in these verses:

"Before Solomon were marshalled his troops of *jinn* and men and birds; and they were all lined in orderly ranks. At length, when they came to a valley of ants, one ant said: 'Go into your dwellings, ants, lest Solomon and his troops inadvertently crush you.'"[1]

The Prophet Solomon stopped his entire army immediately when he heard the ant, thanked God for this gift, and then took a detour out of concern for these ants. Just think, he was not only one of God's Messengers; he was also a king, wealthy beyond our imagination and the leader of an army of thousands of men, *jinns* and animals. The reaction of Solomon not only serves as an aspirational example; it also reinforces the fact that killing even one of the smallest creatures in the world is forbidden in Islam.

1. The Ant, *Surah An-Naml* (27: 17-18)

The Quran also uses animals on numerous occasions to describe the wonders of nature on which we must ponder and reflect, such as birds spreading their wings to fly: "Do they not see the birds above them, spreading their wings and drawing them in? None but the Lord of Grace holds them up. He sees everything".[2]

It is said that Prophet Muhammad was fond of horses and had cats as pets, too. Having a pet animal is a responsibility – it should be given appropriate shelter, food and rest without neglect, and their owner is held accountable for their well-being. Prophet Muhammad said: "God is kind and likes kindness in all things",[3] and added:

> "A good deed done to an animal is like a good deed done to a human being, while an act of cruelty to an animal is as bad as cruelty to a human being.[4]"

Personally, I consider it a collective responsibility to care for animals, let alone endangered species. Eco-tourism is gaining popularity across the world, with a multitude of organizations serving a variety of purposes. On my thirty-fifth birthday I volunteered at Wildlife SOS's Elephant Care and Conservation Centre in India, where almost 60% of Earth's remaining elephant population live. I experienced a life-changing moment during my first encounter with rescued elephants previously held in captivity. My family and I have fond memories of bathing them, chopping their vegetables to eat and seeing them set off on their evening walk in the wild. The joy of giving opened my eyes to the many different ways of helping our planet Earth and getting my daughter involved from a young age.

2. The Dominion, *Surah Al-Mulk* (67:19)

3. Hadith source: Bukhari

4. Conclusion by Mishkat al-Masabih from the hadith of Bukhari and Muslim

THE P WORD

Some believe that Muslims are offended by pork and pigs. In reality we don't hold a grudge against the animal itself – at the end of the day, they are beautiful and smart creatures of God, with feelings too. Our kids watch Peppa Pig, too!

Having said that, pork is the one meat that has been explicitly forbidden for us to eat in the Quran. For many new Muslims, this can be a bit of a challenge as its derived products have a huge presence in Western and Far Eastern cuisine.

When you look at it logically, scientifically and medically, though, the reasons why it is forbidden (*haram*) to eat make a lot of sense. Here are a few:

- Pigs are scavengers and will eat everything and anything, including dead insects, worms, rotting carcasses, garbage, excreta, and other pigs – their own kind.
- Pork products are loaded with artery-clogging cholesterol and saturated fat. Eat pork regularly and you increase your chances of developing health problems such as heart disease, diabetes, arthritis, osteoporosis, Alzheimer's, asthma and impotence.
- There are many diseases that can be transferred from pigs to humans, particularly parasite infestations – some of which can survive even high cooking temperatures.

If you have a strong bacon craving, you can always opt for *halal* turkey bacon or *halal* beef rashers, *halal* beef/chicken sausages and even *halal* pancetta and chorizo. These days, there are all sorts of alternatives, even vegan ones, for the Muslim palate.

THE CRUELTY-FREE APPROACH TO MEAT

"He creates cattle which give you warmth and other benefits; and from them you obtain food. And you find beauty in them when you drive them home in the evening and when you take them out to pasture in the morning."[1]

I occasionally get a surprised look from some Muslims when they find out that I don't eat meat. They say that there is no such thing as vegetarianism in Islam. That is both true and false. In one sense, vegetarianism is seen as unnecessary in Islam, since we respect animals and slaughter them with minimal cruelty and pain. However, if – like me – you just don't like meat, then you don't have to eat it to be a Muslim!

Vegetarianism is a major aspect of some religions, such as Hinduism, whose followers believe that some animals are sacred, or that people can be reincarnated as animals. There are also people who become vegetarian for animal rights reasons.

In Islam, God has indeed made it lawful for us to consume animal meat – but only when they have been treated the right way. They must be taken care of when they are alive, which means space to roam and the right food to eat, and when they are taken to be slaughtered, it cannot be done in front of other animals so as not to frighten them. Today, however, the meat industry has become a toxic and cruel money-making factory. Animals are kept in cages and confined spaces in which they can't move. They're being fed all sorts and pumped with hormones and chemicals to make them fatter. Their movement is restricted so that they can't burn fat and become too muscly. And then they are slaughtered and stunned in front of one another.

1. The Bee, *Surah an-Nahl* (16:5-6)

When slaughtering animals the *halal* way:

- The person performing the slaughter must mention the name of Allah to begin.
- The jugular vein, carotid artery and windpipe must be cut through with a sharp knife. The swift cutting rapidly disconnects the flow of blood to the nerve of the brain responsible for pain, so the animal loses consciousness immediately with minimised pain.
- Blood should be drained from the body of the carcass for hygienic purposes, as it can become a medium for micro-organisms.

This practice makes Islam one of the most animal-friendly religions; shooting the animal in the head, as commonly practised, is not allowed.

ARE YOUR BEAUTY PRODUCTS *HALAL*?

The meat industry is not the only guilty one – what about animal-testing? Islam stands close to the cause of vegans as it does not approve of product-testing on animals because it is also stressful and harmful to them.

Nowadays, a lot of vegan cosmetics and personal-care brands are labelled as animal-friendly and cruelty-free, meaning they do not test their products on animals. I recommend looking out for these on the PETA website, on their 'Beauty Without Bunnies' page and their free app 'Bunny Free', which records more than 2,600 companies in a searchable shopping database. As a programme designed for compassionate shoppers, its aim is to help save mice, guinea pigs, rats and other animals from a lifetime of suffering. Another similar app I would recommend is the Environmental Working Group's app "EWG's Healthy Living".

6. 'BON APPÉTIT! BISMILLAH'

In Islam, God has set out clear guidelines on what Muslims can and can't eat. As you read earlier, there are certain foods that are encouraged because of their enormous health benefits. Likewise, there are foods and animals that aren't permissible (*haram*) to us for various reasons, including detrimental health effects and uncleanliness!

"He has only forbidden you carrion, blood, the flesh of swine, and that on which a name other than God's has been invoked. But he who is driven by necessity, not intending to transgress nor exceeding his need, incurs no sin. God is much-forgiving, merciful."[1]

All plants, fruits, vegetables, grains and pulses are fine. Cows, goats and sheep are permissible to eat, but as a vegetarian, I'm no expert on meat and advise you to dig deeper in your research!

In regards to seafood, scholars' views slightly diverge but I follow the opinion that we can eat any fish as long as it has scales and it must be alive when caught – I wouldn't eat fish that have died in the water and washed up on shore, who knows what diseases resulted in their death? I would advise you do your own research with regards to the vast array of seafood.

Birds of prey and predators are not permissible to eat. They are usually distinguished by having feathers (*halal*) or talons (*haram*). There are more ways to check if a bird is *halal*, which can get a bit complicated, so in general just remember that chickens, turkeys, pigeons and all small birds are permissible to eat – including their eggs.

1. The Cow, *Surah al-Baqarah* (2:173)

It is important to note that all foods are permissible to consume to save a life or if you're in danger of starving to death. It is our obligation to protect human life.

SHOPPING FOR GROCERIES

Shopping for *halal* food may seem like an absolute minefield right now, and you're not alone in feeling overwhelmed. It is not as difficult as it first appears, though, so go at your own pace and soon you'll be a pro at spotting the *halal* from the *haram*.

Buying *Halal* Meat

If you live in a non-Muslim country, you can buy your *halal* meat from butchers that will very clearly display *halal* signage. If you're in any doubt about their authenticity, you can always ask to check their certification. All *halal* restaurants and butchers should be certified by the relevant body. In the UK, for example, this is either the Halal Food Authority (HFA) or the Halal Monitoring Committee (HMC).

A lot of regular supermarkets in non-Muslim countries also stock *halal* meat, which is labelled as such.

Is *Kosher* the same as *Halal*?

There are similarities between the method of slaughter in both *halal* and *kosher*, which is food prepared according to the requirements of Jewish law.

However, the meats are not blessed in the same way. Unlike for *halal*, *kashrut* (Jewish dietary law) does not require God's name to be said before every slaughter after an initial blessing.

There is a difference of opinion among the scholars as to whether or not Muslims can eat *kosher* meat. So as always it is worth asking a scholar for a personalised recommendation

It is important to note that all foods are permissible to consume to save a life or if you're in danger of starving to death. It is our obligation to protect human life.

based on your situation, for example, it may be easier for you to find *kosher* meat than *halal*.

Watching out for Sneaky Ingredients

As a vegetarian, I'm used to reading labels and I know I'm safe whenever I buy a product with a 'Suitable for Vegetarians' label or logo on it. If it does, I rest assured that there are no animal products in it. This is also a great method for those who want to go to extra lengths to check for unlawful ingredients, such as alcohol, which often sneak their way into seemingly innocent food such as vanilla essence, sauces and more. Not everything has a 'Suitable for Vegetarian' sign on it, though, which makes spotting sneaky ingredients a little trickier. You will find a list of sneaky ingredients to look out for on the book's website.

Eating Out

Even in non-Muslim countries there are tons of *halal* restaurants, so don't think that becoming Muslim means you have to be an outdoor vegan for the rest of your life! You can find them online and with apps or websites like zabihah.com. There are also loads of *halal* food bloggers reviewing the *halal* restaurants in major cities across the globe.

If you're travelling and you can't go online to find a *halal* restaurant, a good idea is to find a mosque. A mosque means Muslims, which means finding your way to *halal* restaurants and groceries.

If you really can't find a *halal* restaurant, then just order vegetarian or seafood options, while being mindful of alcohol in your dish. Waiters are used to customers with odd diets and allergies so don't feel embarrassed to ask if there's any meat or alcohol in your dish of choice and if the chef can prepare it without.

Etiquette of Eating

There are several habits recorded of the Prophet during mealtimes that have health benefits attached to them, including not eating fruit directly after meals. Instead, fruit should be eaten just before or between meals. When fruit is eaten close to a meal, especially right after a larger meal and combined with other foods, it's held in the stomach for too long with other foods and will ferment in the gut.

Also, the Prophet would start his meals in the name of God (by saying *Bismillah*, meaning 'by the name of God'); always ate with his right hand and sitting down; shared the food even if there was only a little; would never complain about the food and was appreciative of every morsel.

When I was a child, my parents taught me to wish a good meal and a good appetite to others sitting at the table. In France, we are taught to say '*Bon appétit'* before our first bite. So now, I teach my daughter to say both '*Bon appétit*!' and '*Bismillah'* to bless the food to make sure we have ticked all the boxes!

Narratives about the etiquette of drinking are extremely detailed. Even if plain water was all he had, the Prophet advised his followers to avoid drinking directly from the container or blowing into it, to breathe between sips and to praise God at the end (by saying *Alhamdulillah*, meaning 'all praise is due to God alone'). If you have a baby, note that it is also advised not to blow on their food in order to avoid contamination (one of the numerous things I learned as a new mum!).

The Prophet Muhammad and his companions would eat in extreme moderation, as other Prophets have in the past. Overeating was virtually unheard of. If a person had more food than they needed, they would invite the poor and hungry to join them.

Avoiding overeating isn't just about being mindful of those who are going without, though. Excessive eating is linked to health problems, laziness and wastefulness as well.

"Eat and drink, but do not be wasteful. Surely He does not love the wasteful."[1]

Prophet Muhammad also recommended that we only eat when hungry and to fill just one third of our stomach with food.[2]

Alcohol, smoking and other intoxicants

Alcohol and narcotics are strictly forbidden in Islam. The reasons why are pretty obvious: as intoxicants, they cloud your judgement, can cause you to lose your senses and do all sorts of embarrassing things, are addictive and bad for your health. Islam encourages us to be responsible beings and discourages the use of whatever makes us lose control of our actions.

Most scholars also agree that smoking – tobacco, shisha or marijuana – is discouraged.

1. The Heights, *Surah al-Araf* (7:31)

2. Hadith source: ibn Majah

7. MENTAL HEALTH

Keeping a healthy mind is just as – if not more – important than keeping a healthy body. We've talked a lot about being active and eating well and we will talk about sleeping well, too.

A strong, happy and content mind is a massive part of maintaining a healthy and positive life. So how do we do it?

Well for starters, as Muslims, we're lucky in that we believe in a higher power that has control over our lives. Submitting ourselves to God and His will is a good way to keep stress levels low and is incredibly liberating. Once we give ourselves over to God and put all our faith and trust in Him, we can stop worrying about things we have little to no control over. You might hear the phrase *Insha'Allah*, basically meaning 'God willing' – we put our trust in Him and He will provide what is best for us.

Being the complex creatures that we are, we probably will keep worrying, even though logically we know we shouldn't.

When this happens, prayer and invocation are a good way to keep connected with God, to empty our hearts to Him and remind ourselves that He has a plan for us.

TRIALS AND EMOTIONS

God says in the Quran, "that it is He who causes people to laugh and weep."[1]

Did you know that smiling is actually a form of charity in Islam? This proves it can affect others positively! Making people happy, being good to others and smiling are all traits of the ideal Muslim.

1. *Surah An-Najm* (53:43)

That doesn't mean that you're not allowed to be upset. Islam recognises sadness and depression – and the distinction between the two. In fact, even the Prophet was said to have experienced all sorts of emotions, including profound anxiety, through all kinds of trials.

"We shall certainly try you with a certain measure of fear and hunger, and with diminution of wealth, lives and crops. But give glad tidings to those who remain patient in adversity."[2] God later says in the Quran, "Do people think that once they say: 'We are believers', they will be left alone and not put to a test?"[3]

According to some narrations, the short chapter 'The Morning Hours' (*Surah Al Duha*) was revealed to the Prophet when there was a brief lag in revelations. He was said to be anxiously awaiting a revelation in a difficult situation. This chapter begins with two oaths and then informs Prophet Muhammad of the good news that God has not forsaken him. It adds that soon God will provide for him so abundantly that he will become content. This applies to all of us:

"By the bright morning hours, and the night when it grows still and dark, your Lord has neither forsaken you, nor does He hate you. Surely the life to come will be better for you than this present life. And, certainly, in time your Lord will be bounteous to you and you will be well pleased. Has He not found you an orphan and given you a shelter? And found you in error, and guided you? And found you poor and enriched you?"[4]

This entire chapter of the Quran can be considered a direct remedy from God for sadness, as with praying, making invocations, remembering God and doing good deeds. If God is the one who gives us sadness and hardship, then He is the only one who can take it away.

2. The Cow, *Surah Al Baqarah* (2:155)

3. The Spider, *Surah Al-'Ankabut* (29:2)

4. The Morning Hours, *Surah Ad-Duhaa* (93:1-8)

Grab your copy of the Quran to read the full speech in Luqman's chapter, surah 31

In Islam, we are always encouraged to reach out to God and speak to him in both good and bad times. There is a narration in the chapter 'Solace' that states that with every hardship comes ease, and as Muslims we need to hold on to that thought and be patient whenever we're going through a difficult time.[1] Patience is a key to happiness; in fact, it is mentioned ninety times in the Quran. It narrates the time when Prophet Luqman gave valuable life lessons to his son in a heartfelt speech and advised him to "endure with fortitude whatever befalls you".[2] How could we appreciate tears of joy if we hadn't tasted those of sorrow, and how would we have hope when feeling down if we hadn't lived moments of blissful happiness? Counting our blessings, however small, truly helps transform negative feelings into a state of gratitude. Did you know that positive self-talk is also said to trick the brain into feeling happier? Journaling is also a commonly used method to train our mind on how to focus on the good things in our life – and the best part is, writing is practically free!

DEPRESSION AND MENTAL HEALTH

Until recently, mental health problems and depression were viewed as a taboo topic in a lot of Muslim communities that just didn't want to recognise them as actual diseases. Even mainstream society has a hard time accepting that depression is a real illness.

The population of the Middle East and North Africa has one of the highest rates of clinical depression around the world. Unsurprisingly, Afghanistan and Palestine are at the top of the list.

According to the World Health Organisation, clinical depression is, "A mental disorder, characterised by sadness, loss of interest or pleasure, feelings of guilt or low self-worth, disturbed sleep or appetite, feelings of tiredness, and poor concentration".

1. Solace, *Surah Ash-Sharh* (94:5-6)

2. Luqman (31:17)

> Be patient in **adversity**, for **God** is with those who are patient in adversity.[3]

Islam recognised it as an illness since its early beginnings – and, as with any illness, it should be treated with professional or medical help. At the same time, Muslims who suffer from depression are encouraged to pray more, connect more with God and ask Him for help and peace. Daily meditation and prayer is said to boost self-confidence and optimism and lead to increased activity in the prefrontal cortex, which helps regulate emotions and decrease stress. According to research conducted at Wayne State University, there is a positive correlation between a patient's faith and improved emotional and physical rehabilitation outcomes. Believing in a benevolent, loving higher power is a source of healing to those who feel completely hopeless and helpless.

Similarly, reading the Quran can provide consolation as the verses and stories within it (such as the lives of the Prophets Joseph, Abraham, Job and Jonah) can be a source of hope and inspiration.

Whatever trials you are facing, always remember that God Himself has said that no one besides Him can rescue a soul from hardship, and with hardship follows ease. He has sent us a Divine prayer in the Quran: "Our Lord! Do not punish us if we forget or make a mistake. Our Lord! Do not place a burden on us like the one you placed on those before us. Our Lord! Do not burden us with what we cannot bear. Pardon us, forgive us, and have mercy on us. You are our (only) Guardian. So grant us victory over the disbelieving people."[4]

Try and hold onto your faith, no matter what the difficulty, and use your trials as a means to become closer to God.

3. The Spoils of War, *Surah Al-Anfal* (8:46)

4. The Cow, *Surah Al Baqarah* (2:286)

FOCUS ON TODAY, NOT TOMORROW

The belief in one God, all-knowing and all-ruling, is at the very core of Islam. Anything that detracts from this is forbidden – and this includes zodiac signs, astrology, superstition and fortune tellers. As fun as it may be to read your star sign, even if you think you don't believe in what you read, it can play with your mind. Besides, once again we should be responsible and in full control of our own lives rather than seeking what we've been predicted. We've all done it – read a column that predicted something that happened to come true and then started to wonder if astrology really could predict the future.

It is God who determines the course of our lives – not the stars.

Likewise, going to fortune tellers, tarot readers or anyone else claiming to know what the future holds is wrong. Don't be fooled by people claiming to be religious clerics who are also dabbling in fortune-telling – this is strictly forbidden in Islam. It is God alone who knows what our future holds – not fortune tellers – and trying to meddle in His affairs means that we're not placing our trust in Him.

SLEEP AND DREAMS

Good health (both mental and physical) and good sleep go hand-in-hand. If you think about it, how many hours of sleep turn into days and months in our lives? Prophet Muhammad has taught us sleeping positions, protective prayers against insomnia, and warned us about dreams and nightmares.

In Islam, there are three types of dreams:

1. visions or dreams that come from God.
2. dreams that are from Satan to frighten us or cause us distress.
3. the workings of the subconscious.

There are various narrations explaining what we should do after experiencing a 'good' or 'bad' dream.

A good dream:

- We should praise God for the good dream.
- We should talk about it to those whom we love and who have our best interest at heart.

A bad dream:

- We should seek refuge with God from evil by reciting: "I seek God's protection against Satan, the accursed one" (*A'udhu billahi min ash-shaytaan ir-rajeem*).
- When we wake up from the nightmare, we should 'spit' three times to the left – without actually spitting saliva (it's more the motion, really!).
- It is preferable not to mention the nightmare to anyone – unless you feel it may be hiding a symbolic meaning and would feel reassured with a valid interpretation. Again, finding a righteous person to talk to with experience is key.

KEEP BUSY AND BALANCED

They say an idle mind is a devil's workshop – and I agree! It is important to keep busy, not just so you don't fall into a habit of laziness but so you feel fulfilled and accomplished as well. Islam encourages moderation – so whatever you do, try and maintain a balance between your work/education, your spouse, your family, your friends, your social life, your 'me time' and, most importantly, your faith. If for some reason you don't feel centered, as if there's an imbalance somewhere, try to work out what is throwing you off and how you can combat it.

CHAPTER

3 WOMANKIND

"And live with them in kindness"[1]

Let's talk about the elephant in the room: the status of women in Islam. I want to delve deep into the subject. The way we are most commonly portrayed – as 'oppressed' by the veil, or by men, as terrorists, or as being deprived of education – is quite upsetting to us Muslim women. While all these stereotypes can be found in a minority of cases, Islam as a religion does not approve of such treatment of women and the religion's values stand far beyond these mischaracterisations.

1. Excerpt from Women, *Surah An-Nisa* (4:19)

When *Elle* magazine asked her about western ignorance concerning Islamic women, Queen Rania Al Abdullah of Jordan said:

"When I travel abroad, I'm always astonished and touched by the wrong interpretations concerning Muslim women.
For example, being a feminist and a Muslim is not a contradiction in terms. In the history of Islam, for example – and many Westerners will not be aware of this – there are numerous examples of influential women in the political, scientific, military, business and industrial domains.
Islam gives women many rights.
Nowadays, the greatest challenges for Muslim women with regard to rights and equality are not situated in the religious arena where they are granted rights, but in the social and cultural arenas.
We cannot judge the reality of millions of Muslim women by watching short items on the television or reading the headlines. It is necessary to make the effort to approach them, to speak to them, to listen to their life stories."

Most importantly, what lies beneath the 'Muslim woman' label, the veil or the modest clothing is the right to be respected with dignity, the entitlement to education, the freedom to choose her life partner, the strength to care for others and to look after herself. There isn't one type of Muslim woman; we come in all shades – rich or poor, single or married – and we're all beautiful in our own way, with our own stories, strengths and flaws. We are generous with our friends, kind-hearted with strangers, but we also have a sense of humour. We are capable, ambitious, and, like all other women in the world, we are each unique.

Did you know that we have an entire chapter dedicated to us in the Quran? *An-nisa*, literally meaning 'women' in Arabic, was revealed entirely in the presence of Prophet Muhammad's wife Aisha over a span of ten years. She became an expert in feminine Islamic jurisprudence as she knew and understood the causes and circumstances of the revelations. She would ask her husband for detailed interpretations of this chapter, in which God talks about a variety of social issues: adopting orphans and their rights, marriage, women's rights to wealth and inheritance, widows, women's reputations, adultery, and much more.

Her methodology in the interpretation of the Holy Quran has become the foundation from which today's scholars study it in accordance with the teachings of the Prophet, which are known as *sunnah* and *hadiths*. Scholars use her methodology to issue rulings called *fatwas*.

She is also one of the most prolific narrators of the Prophet's teachings, with 2,210 narrations, starting with their marital life, and she quickly became an expert in other social, economic and political fields. Her home in Madinah became a study centre where other famous narrators, renowned scholars and students would come to learn, listen and study.

1. THE CREATION OF (WO)MANKIND

ADAM AND EVE: THE ORIGINAL PAIR

It all started when God created the very first man: Adam. Before Adam, there were only the angels and *jinns*. Iblis (who is better known as Satan, or *Shaytan* in Arabic) was a *jinn* who held an elevated rank among the angels for his devoted worship to God.

God breathed a soul into Adam and presented him to the angels and *jinn*, asking them to prostrate before him. They all did so, except for Iblis who, full of arrogance, refused to show his respect and follow the command of God. He argued that *jinns*, who were created from fire, were superior to man, who was formed from clay.

God replied: "Off with you hence! It is not for you to show your arrogance here. Get out, then; you will always be among the humiliated."[1]

Iblis asked God to allow him respite until the Day of Resurrection, which was granted to him. As told to us in the Quran, Iblis said: "Since you let me fall in error, I shall indeed lurk in ambush for them all along Your straight path, and I shall most certainly fall upon them from the front and from the rear, and from their right and from their left; and You will find most of them ungrateful".[2] God replied that whoever followed Satan would go to Hell.

Meanwhile in Heaven, God was creating a partner for Adam from the man's rib – a woman known as Eve, or *Hawwa* in Arabic (which derives from the word 'living'). God warned Adam and Eve about the devil, declaring him to be

1. The Heights, *Surah Al-A'raf* (7:13)

2. The Heights, *Surah Al-A'raf* (7:17)

mankind's biggest enemy. He also asked them not to touch a particular tree there in Paradise.

This was the perfect opportunity for Satan to exploit the weakness of human nature and persuade both Adam and Eve to go against God's instructions: "They both ate of its fruit; and thereupon their shameful parts became visible to them, and they began to cover themselves with pieced-together leaves from the Garden. Thus did Adam disobey his Lord, and thus did he stray into error. Then his Lord elected him [for His grace], accepted his repentance, and bestowed His guidance upon him."[3]

This is the original story, as described in the Quran.

THE ORIGINAL SIN: A CHRISTIAN DOCTRINE

In the Bible, Eve is solely responsible for giving in to the devil's seductions: "And it was not Adam who was deceived, but the woman being deceived, fell into transgression."[4]

She then tempted Adam into eating the fruit, thereby setting the precedent for all women to be seen as temptresses, and all mankind as inherently sinful.

Another verse speaks of the ramifications of her sin: "To the woman He (God) said, 'I will greatly multiply your pain in childbirth, in pain you will bring forth children; Yet your desire will be for your husband, And he will rule over you.'"[5]

In Christianity, humans are all thought to carry a part of this original sin and so are born sinful beings. For Muslims and Jews, however, babies enter the world as innocent beings, with a pure soul untainted by any evil.

In Islam, we believe that our nature is to submit to God – in other words, we are born Muslims. Hence when children pass away at a young age, they enter Heaven because of their innocence and natural inclination to God. It is also for this

3. Ta-Ha (20:121-122)

4. The Bible, 1 Timothy (2:14)

5. The Bible, Genesis (3:16)

reason that many people say that one 'reverts' rather than 'converts' to Islam – in other words, we return to our natural state, the way we were before our upbringing diverted us from following the true teachings of God.

Furthermore, Islam removes the negative focus on Eve by specifically clarifying that both she and Adam were responsible for their actions. Eve was not weaker than Adam, and their descent on earth was not a punishment or a degradation: this was God's plan and intention from the beginning – for them to understand the tricks of Satan. After they repented, God forgave them both and made Adam a Prophet on earth.

I think it's important to bear in mind this fundamental fact while you read this chapter. It changes everything about how we, women, are perceived – from the moment we come into this world as newborns and as we evolve into womanhood.

FREE WILL AND DESTINY

Adam and Eve perfectly illustrate the question of free will versus destiny. If God had planned all along for them to live on earth, did Adam, Eve and Iblis really have the freedom to choose their actions or were they always destined to make those choices? If God has willed it, His plan will come to fruition eventually. This is why, in Islam, Adam and Eve are ultimately not to blame for their fall and, having repented, they were forgiven for the mistake they did commit.

There is an important distinction to be made between the two. We have the free will to make right or wrong choices, which we will be judged on. Life is like a railway line that splits into many tracks, offering you choices at every turn; you're in the driver's seat – not the passenger seat. It's for this reason that we pray to God to guide us on the straight path.[1]

1. *Surah Al-Fatihah*

However, the choices we make are already written in our destiny. You see, God knows the future of all things and we are His creation, so He knows us better than we know our own selves. It's like knowing exactly how your child will react to x, y or z. In the same way, He knows our next move and He knows its consequences.

As God says in the Quran, "No incident can take place, either on earth or in yourselves, unless it be recorded in a decree before We bring it into being – that is easy for God."[2]

"With Him are the keys to what lies beyond the reach of human perception: none knows them but Him. He knows all that the land and sea contain; not a leaf falls but He knows it; and neither is there a grain in the earth's deep darkness, nor anything fresh or dry but is recorded in a clear book."[3]

However, even if you have decided to do something, it will not happen unless God has willed it – this is the reason why Muslims always say *insha'Allah*, meaning 'if God wills it', to remind ourselves that our fate is in His hands. As He further describes in the Quran: "Yet, you cannot will except by the Will of God, Lord of all the worlds."[4]

It is a reminder that what God has decreed will eventually happen – even death. God says: "Wherever you may be death will overtake you, even though you be in towers built up strong and high."[5]

It is also necessary to point out that we are responsible for our own actions, and we are not held responsible for our ancestors', parents', children's, or anybody else's actions. The mistakes committed by Adam and Eve therefore do not interfere with our lives. God says in the Quran: "For he who commits a sin, does so to his own hurt. God is indeed all-knowing, wise. But he who commits a fault or a sin and throws the blame therefore on an innocent person, burdens himself with both falsehood and a flagrant sin."[6]

2. Iron, *Surah Al-Hadid* (57:22)

3. Cattle, *Surah al-An'am* (6:59)

4. The Darkening, *Surah At-Takwir* (81:29)

5. Excerpt from Women, *Surah An-Nisa* (4:78)

6. Women, *Surah An-Nisa* (4:111-112)

GENDER EQUALITY AND DIVERSITY

The idea that Islam is inherently oppressive of women is one of the mainstream media's most harmful mischaracterisations. Of course, forms of prejudice and oppression do exist in some Islamic countries, but they are certainly not limited to the Islamic world – and, in fact, Islam itself condemns such behaviour.

Gender inequality is a global issue. Women from all walks of life face discrimination from their male counterparts: a woman CEO may face resistance and prejudice; a Hollywood actress may experience sexual harassment. On the flip side, in Islam women can gain elected office and become leaders through sports, arts, science and more.

There is a Chinese proverb that says: "He who asks a question remains a fool for five minutes. He who does not ask remains a fool forever." In Islam, we can question everything and ask scholars anything – we're not told to accept information blindly. It is narrated that the Prophet said, "Seeking knowledge is an obligation upon every Muslim".[1] In the Quran, God encourages women, like men, to seek knowledge, to travel as a means to exploring His creation.

Islam recognises diversity between men and women, since God did not create us alike. However, this does not entail nor justify any mistreatment – we are not labeled as less capable than our opposite gender. The Prophet Muhammad said, "God enjoins you to treat women well, for they are your mothers, daughters, aunts"; and added, "A good man treats women with honour".[2] Given that he said this at a time when women had no rights at all, we can see that the Prophet took the treatment of women seriously. This extended to his domestic life: it was narrated that the Prophet said of his deceased wife, Khadija, that he was "nourished by her love".[3]

1. Hadith source: Sunan al-Bayhaqi
2. Hadith source: Tirmidhi
3. Hadith source: Muslim

The advent of Islam gave women rights that were previously unheard of in society and they gained the right to education; to buy, sell and trade/work; to own property and manage their own finances; to choose when to marry and whom to marry; and to initiate their own divorce.

Some patriarchal societies are still perpetuating un-Islamic traditions and treating women unfairly. Sometimes non-Muslims choose to see only these misogynistic actions and equate them to Islam. Such horrors as honour killings, forced marriages, domestic violence and female circumcision are not Islamic. These crimes should be a source of concern for each of us today; it is our duty to help those women whose rights are not being granted or respected.

God declares in the Quran that He created us from a single soul[4] and neither has superiority over the other on the basis of gender – a brother over his sister, a son over his mother, a husband over his wife. As women we are given personhood in our own right and we do not gain an identity through our relationship to a man – neither do we need to imitate a man in order to gain respect.

In Islam, the only clear distinction is that made between believers and disbelievers – not men and women. Both genders will be judged and treated equally on the Day of Judgement: "For all men and women who have submitted themselves to God – all believing men and believing women, all truly devout men and truly devout women, all men and women who are true to their word, all men and women who are patient in adversity, all men and women who humble themselves before God, all men and women who give in charity, all men and women who fast, all men and women who are mindful of their chastity, and all men and women who always remember God – for them all God has prepared forgiveness of sins and a mighty reward".[5] In fact, the Quran uses a variety of different terms to address both genders as one, such as "O humanity!", "O Children of Adam", "O people of intelligence".

4. Women, *Surah An-Nisa* (4:1)

5. The Confederates, *Surah Al-Ahzab* (33:35)

I will never deny of you – male or female – the rewards for your deeds. Both are equal in reward.[1]

We, Muslim women are also encouraged to reach the full potential of our character and morality in order to excel in society. However, balance in our practice and piety is important. Once, the Prophet Muhammad was questioned about standing all night in prayer and fasting all day – it seemed impossible for the followers who tried to reciprocate his example. He replied: "Do not do that. Sleep and stand (in prayer); fast and break your fast. For your eyes have a right over you, your body has a right over you, your wife has a right over you, your guest has a right over you, and your friend has a right over you."

HOW MUSLIM MEN SHOULD TREAT WOMEN

It's as simple as this: "The best men are those who are best to their wives," as Prophet Muhammad told his followers. As an incentive, he told them that he who offered a gift to his wife would be rewarded just as if he had given in charity.[2]

The Prophet urged men to treat all women with kindness – not only their wives, but also their mothers, daughters, nieces, cousins, co-workers, neighbours – and the list goes on: "O Muslims! I advise you to be gentle with women, for they are created from a rib, and the most curved portion of the rib is its upper part. If you try to straighten it, it will break, and if you leave it, it will remain curved; so I urge you to take care of the woman."[3]

1. Hadith source: Tirmidhi
2. Hadith source: Muslim
3. Hadith source: Bukhari

The Quran says spouses "are a garment for you, as you are for them."[4] This clearly shows the complimentary nature that God intended for husbands and wives, particularly since the Quran further reveals that God created us and everything else in pairs.[5] Why would our relationship be described as a garment? If you think about it, our clothes are multi-functional – their primary role is to conceal our body and private parts in the same way that our partner hides our defects. They're also the closest thing to our skin throughout the day and night, and they're an extension of our personality. They can make us look better – or worse! They're also a source of comfort against the elements. Can you think of anything that is closer to you than garments? Well, God describes our relationship with Him as even closer in the verse: "It is We who have created man, and We know what his soul whispers to him and We are closer to him than his jugular vein."[6]

When entering the Muslim community, it might be surprising or even awkward for a western woman to see a Muslim man avoiding prolonged eye contact. At first, I was a little offended and intrigued by this behaviour, until I realised it is actually a sign of modesty on their behalf and ultimately, respect. Men are advised to lower their gaze in their interactions with women and I've learned to appreciate their mindfulness.

In Islam, it is a man's duty to take care of the household's needs and obligations. A father's responsibility is to bear the cost of the mother's and children's food and clothing, on a reasonable basis. It is their primary role in the family.[7]

Of course, today, women are increasingly becoming the family breadwinner – and this can add a lot of weight on our shoulders and introduce more stress to a relationship. It can be difficult to find the right balance between work and spending time with family.

4. The Cow, *Surah al-Baqarah* (2: 187)

5. The Tidings, *Surah An-Naba* (78: 8)

6. *Qaf* (50: 16–17)

7. The Cow, *Surah al-Baqarah* (2: 233)

I remember having to travel abroad frequently for work while I was pregnant and also having to return to the office shortly after giving birth. Needless to say, having a full-time job while still breastfeeding, looking after an infant, spending time with my husband, speaking to my parents on Skype and trying to meet up with friends was strenuous. At the end of the day, though, being an active and responsible woman gave me a great sense of accomplishment and fulfilment – I had made that choice. Thank God my husband was supportive, as I couldn't have done it without him.

Despite what some may think, a working woman is compatible with Islam – in fact, Khadija, the Prophet's first wife, was a successful businesswoman. Couples should discuss and come to a mutual agreement that suits their individual circumstances in the sanctity of love and respect for their marriage. We are first and foremost responsible for our household and for giving our children a good education – that is the primary role of women in Islam's family dynamics.

THE STRENGTH OF FAMILY TIES

Within family dynamics, we should also strive to be good mothers, wives and daughters. These acts of kindness and good deeds are continuously rewarded throughout a woman's life:

- As a daughter, we will open the door to Heaven for our father.
- As a wife, our life partner completes half of our faith and we complete his.
- As a mother, Paradise lies under our feet.

In Islam, our parents are put on a pedestal – if family is golden, parents are diamonds. The Quran repeatedly encourages us to take care of them into their old age. Our gratitude towards them should be endless – simply the fact that our mother carried us in her womb and went through pain to bring us into the world is enough to be forever indebted to her. This high status given to mothers is very unique to Islam. On top of this, both of the parents' sleepless nights, their role in educating us and their moral guidance can never be repaid.

The Quran says, "Your Lord has ordained that you shall worship none but Him, and that you must be kind to your parents. Should one of them, or both, attain to old age in your care, never say 'Ugh' to them or chide them, but always speak gently and kindly to them, and spread over them humbly the wings of your tenderness, and say, 'My Lord, bestow on them Your grace, even as they reared and nurtured me when I was a child".[1] So keep that in mind next time your mum asks you to install an app on her phone!

The status given to parents also applies to grandparents. Even after their death, we should continue to pray for God's mercy on them and give charity on their behalf.

I know many people whose dysfunctional relationships with their parents rekindled after converting to Islam, even if their parents had not given them the love, support and kindness that all children deserve. As Muslims, we shouldn't completely cut off relations with any relatives.

1. The Night Journey, *Surah Al-Isra* (17:23-24)

2. WOMEN'S RIGHTS

When the Quran was revealed, Islam was revolutionary in all social aspects, not least in the realm of women's rights. Before Islam, women were literally seen as bad omens in many superstitious traditions. Now, men had to learn to appreciate women and respect them.

We've already covered the fact that, in Islam, knowledge is a must. We also know that Aisha, the wife of the Prophet, was very knowledgeable when it came to Islamic jurisprudence and was an advocate for women to be granted the rights attributed to them in the Quran. She was engaged in defending the equal values, equity and dignity prescribed to women in Islam. Her feminism was a fruit of the revelations to both men and women to do good and bring justice to the world, which led her to eventually become a political figure. So, what are some of those rights?

SHARIA LAW

The term is intimidating, even frightening to many people – but what does it really mean? Just as Jews submit to the jurisdiction of Rabbinic courts and Christians submit to Christian Conciliation tribunals, Muslims have *sharia*. But it is important to note that in the end, the national law presides.

Sharia is the religious law taken from Islamic tradition – namely the Quran and teachings of the Prophet. The principles are based on fairness, bringing justice, eliminating prejudice and alleviating hardship. The Prophet delivered different judgements depending on the context, so there is no one-size-fits-all judgement. Jurists must be deeply versed in the Quran and *sunnah* to issue a verdict.

American jurist Abed Awad explains: "*Sharia* is more than simply law in the perspective sense, it is also the methodology through which a jurist engages the foundational religious texts (Quran and *sunnah*) to search for Divine will. As a jurist-made law, the outcome of the process of ascertaining Divine will is called *fiqh*, which is the moral and legal anchor of a Muslim's total existence. Everything from what the Muslims eat, to how they treat animals and protect the environment, to the way they conduct commercial trade, to the way they solemnise their marriage and to the way their estate must be distributed at death is governed by *Sharia*, for *Sharia* dictates every aspect of an observant Muslim's moral life. Therefore, *Sharia* is extremely personal to the majority of Muslims regardless of their level of religiosity."

TEN GROUND-BREAKING SHARIA LAWS THAT IMPROVED WOMEN'S STATUS AFTER THE RISE OF ISLAM

In the seventh century, before Islam, women were considered objects.

1 Women are entitled to inherit wealth.

Women have the right to choose their husband and to refuse a marriage proposal, and so cannot be forced into marriage. Furthermore, they have the right to initiate divorce. 2

3 The dowry is paid directly to the bride and not to her male relatives.

Regulations defined marriage as part of a contract between a man and a woman. 4

5 Female infanticide is strictly forbidden and a punishable act. Baby girls are considered a blessing.

Men must financially support their wives – even, for a short period, after divorce. 6

7 Married women have full control of their own money, and can choose to contribute to the household expenses as they wish. Women also have full control of their property.

Women have the right to keep their own family name after they marry. 8

9 They have the right to vote and express their opinions publically.

They also have the right to work (or not) and to hold a leadership position. 10

3. MODESTY

"Modesty is the best jewel of a woman" – so said Fatima, the Prophet's daughter. In Arabic, we use the word *haya* to talk about modesty. It's a powerful word, embodying a concept of modesty that goes beyond the way we dress. As well as dressing respectfully, it is mandatory for Muslims – both men and women – to clothe ourselves in self-respect, honour and humility. Modesty of character and conduct is as important as our physical appearance: while both genders have been given a standard of dress encouraging us to cover parts of our bodies, we must also try to avoid arrogance, vanity and pride.

A MODEST AND HUMBLE NATURE

"Children of Adam, We have sent down to you clothing to cover your nakedness, and garments pleasing to the eye; but the robe of God-fearingness is the finest of all. In this there is a sign from God, so that they may reflect."[1]

When I was growing up, the Virgin Mary was the epitome of modesty for me, as were the nuns who had taught me at school. Their clothes are an outward expression of the characteristics they embody – piety, kindness and humility – and invoke respect in others. You wouldn't address a nun disrespectfully, would you?

Similarly, God says in the Quran: "Prophet! Say to your wives, daughters and all believing women that they should draw over themselves some of their outer garments. This will be more conducive to their being recognised and not affronted. God is much-forgiving, ever-merciful."[2]

My understanding, from reading the Quran, is that God pairs character together with appearance to achieve

1. The Heights, *Surah Al-A'raf* (7:26)

2. The Confederates, *Surah Al-Ahzab* (33:59)

> The true servants of the Lord of Grace are those who walk gently on earth, and who, whenever the ignorant address them, say peace.[3]

modesty and humility – the true meaning of *hijab*. Hijabis (a term commonly used to describe Muslim women who in following this principle cover their hair) consider the veil another way of connecting spiritually with God. It represents an inner devotion that is unique to every one of them. From my personal experience, I can also testify that wearing a headscarf does not make a woman more pious over another – don't judge a book by its cover!

3. The Criterion, *Surah Al-Furqan* (25:63)

Today, the headscarf is also an element of cultural dress in many countries and stems from a specific tradition of modesty. In some secular countries, like France, it is an icon of the Islamic faith and has been banned in schools and universities; the burkini (modest swimwear for covered women) has been banned from beaches.

While Muslim women should dress modestly, they shouldn't be forced to wear the hijab if they don't feel ready, or if they choose not to.

DRESSING MODESTLY: AN ACQUIRED HABIT

A first step towards dressing modestly is realising that we can incorporate the concept of modesty and humility into our own cultural and personal identity – there is no set Islamic uniform. Modesty, and *hijab* specifically, spark differing views and it is best to find out more for yourself which parts of the body to cover and discuss with trusted scholars.

New Muslims are often put under a lot of pressure when it comes to the way we dress and we are judged from all sides: Muslims tend to judge us if we dress differently to their particular understanding of *hijab* and may not appreciate how far we have come.

While non-Muslim friends and family members may criticise us or comment on our choice to dress differently than we used to. Trust me, I've been there! We all have – learning more, responding respectfully towards others and giving ourselves time are the answer.

If you're in this situation, my advice as a veteran is – as always – to do things progressively and at your own pace. To adhere to changes and new practices in your life in line with your beliefs and relationship with God. After all, our actions should only be to please *Him* – not *His creation*. As new Muslims we feel euphoria in the beginning and may be too keen to adopt new practices too soon, then letting them go too quickly. Achieving modesty is a journey I am still on today, as it doesn't come as naturally for some people as it does for others, who were taught at a young age to dress respectfully at all times. Certain changes are easier than others, everybody is different!

As for the headscarf – also known as *sheila* or veil and commonly referred to in everyday language as *hijab*– it isn't unique to Islam. It is a form of religious or cultural dress in several other cultures – even women in the West were still wearing headscarves up until the early twentieth century. In fact, both my grand-mothers did whenever they went out, as was the tradition for ladies in France.

Within Islam, the majority see the headscarf as an embodiment of the modesty Muslim women strive for. It empowers us by allowing us to show others only what we choose to, preserving the rest for our family. Of course, differences of opinion exist and you're entitled to develop your own. In fact, Muslim women who are not yet ready or choose not to cover their hair will usually follow other tenets of modesty, such as wearing loose, non-revealing clothing to hide their curves.

BECOMING A *HIJABI*

Choosing to wear *hijab* is a long-term commitment not to be taken lightly. It is a way of life; an extension of your personality, demeanour and behaviour. Putting on the veil feels like getting into character: when you wear the veil, you also wear politeness, humility, and all the positive values that Islam represents. It is also a huge responsibility as it makes you a visible ambassador for Islam.

The idea that the headscarf is oppressive to women, or that we are all forced to wear it, is offensive to the vast majority of Muslim women. Most *hijabis* feel empowered to cover and consciously go against the mainstream objectification and sexualisation of women. My sister-in-law, for example, decided to start wearing *hijab* when she was a teenager in France. Shortly afterwards, France banned the wearing of headscarves in public. Where is the freedom in that? Wearing her *hijab* had instilled in my sister-in-law the drive to excel in all aspects of her life. To me, it feels oppressive to take that away from her.

Let's clear one thing up straight away: women don't wear their headscarf at home and we don't sleep with it on! It is only worn when we leave the house. At home, around our husbands and families, we can wear whatever we want.

We also cover when offering our ritual prayer (*salah*) to God and, to preserve our dignity, we will be fully covered when we go to our graves.

There are many ways of wearing your headscarf. Go ahead and experiment to find ways that make you feel comfortable and suit your face shape and personal style. There's loads of great advice and inspiration online, including YouTube tutorial videos that can teach you different ways to style your headscarf. Remember to experiment with colour, too; you can hold fabrics swatches next to your face to see which shades are most flattering.

Just as there are countless styles and colours of headscarves, the materials used to make headscarves vary – you might prefer to wear silk, georgette, cotton, jersey, or polyester.

Some are thicker and more suitable for winter (you won't need ear muffs!), some are more breathable for the heat and humidity of warmer countries, and others are even embellished with Swarovski crystals for *Eid* and weddings.

FASHION AND #THEMODESTYMOVEMENT

Unless you're shopping at specialist stores, it can feel impossible to find the perfect modest fit – the dress is too short, the shirt is too see-through, the trousers are too tight... You might need or want to buy some accessories to help you dress modestly. Rest assured, just a few inexpensive additions to your wardrobe can make your life a lot easier!

Modesty sleeves

Think of these as 'instant sleeves'! Made from elasticated material, they're super-easy to slip over your arms to make sure you're covered, even in a shorter sleeved shirt or loose-sleeved kaftan.

Underscarves

One of the most easy-to-wear essentials is the underscarf. It looks a little like a cap or a turban and you wear it like a head-band underneath your headscarf to prevent the scarf from slipping backwards. It also helps you to make sure your hair isn't showing, especially at the forehead. As an added bonus, it ensures full coverage even if you're wearing a sheer *hijab*. Underscarves come in many materials, from lycra, viscose and polyester to Egyptian cotton, some more fashionable and some more breathable. You can even mix and match the colours of your underscarves and headscarves for a trendy look. It all comes down to what suits you best, and what makes you feel most confident.

Pins

An alternative to wearing an underscarf or tucking in the sides of your *hijab* is using a pin to secure your headscarf in place. You can use anything from a safety pin to a fashionable brooch.

However, the fashion world is changing. Modest fashion is making waves, with haute-couture designers adopting the *abaya* and *hijab* on the runway, modest fashion shows in New York, Paris and Dubai, and Muslim women becoming top models, like Halima Aden, who wore her *hijab* on the cover of Vogue Arabia. Sports brands now sell *hijabs* with breathable fabric for aspiring athletes, and there's even a *hijab*-wearing Barbie doll, based on Olympic fencer Ibtihaj Muhammed!

Brands simply can no longer ignore the presence and spending power of Muslim women – and the importance of representation.

"The modesty movement is amazing because it's not just reaching out to Muslims all over the world; it's even reaching out to non-Muslims as well," says Mariah Idrissi, who was the world's first *hijab*-wearing model. "For women who choose to cover for religious reasons, it's more than just a trend, it's a lifestyle."

Ghizlan Guenez, CEO and founder of The Modist, an online modest fashion retailer, told Vogue: "There are misconceptions about what modesty is. I think that when you speak to modesty, sometimes there are certain perceptions that modesty is this certain religion, this certain region, a particular age and particular look. We want to change those perceptions. We are saying that modesty can be so many different things, can be coveted by so many different women, and that it can be cool and beautiful and elegant and everything a woman wants."

HEROINES OF THE GOLDEN AGE

History has forgotten many a woman's discovery – or given the credit to men instead. Historians and researchers are just starting to right that wrong by digging into archives to unearth the incredible contributions made by women from across the world.

The seventh century heralded the start of an unprecedented period of breakthrough discoveries in the world of science and medicine. Many Muslim women left their mark during this time, and we remember them as 'Heroines of the Golden Age'. Mariam Al-Asturlabi, a Syrian woman, contributed to the invention of astrolabes (an astronomical instrument); Turkish princess Gevher Nesibe Sultan endowed a hospital complex housing a school dedicated to medical studies and a mosque; in Sub-Saharan Africa, Queen Amina of Zaria founded a kingdom and is still remembered for her fierce military exploits; Zaynab Al Shahda was a renowned calligrapher of her time, also celebrated for her work and teachings in Islamic law.

And did you know that the world's oldest library and university was founded by a Muslim woman in the year 859? Fatima Al-Fihri founded the complex in Fez, Morocco as a mosque after inheriting from her beloved merchant father. He had encouraged her as a little girl to pursue her insatiable quest for knowledge. She financed and oversaw the complex's construction and laid the first stone herself. Fatima's mosque would become one of the most respected in town, and reputed scholars travelled from afar to teach at its school, which was soon known as one of the best in the region. It grew into the world's first ever university – the University of Al Qarawiyyin, which is still operational today. It now houses a collection of 4,000 rare books and ancient Arabic manuscripts written by renowned North African scholars, some of whom are women.

AMAZING PIOUS WOMEN IN HISTORY

Asiya – wife of the Pharaoh

Asiya (Bithiah in biblical texts) was an Egyptian queen, considered in Islam to be one of the best of women that ever lived, alongside the likes of the Virgin Mary.[1] She is one of very few people mentioned in the Quran. She was intended as God's example for us, as per the verse: "God has also given examples of believers: Pharaoh's wife, who said: '*My Lord! Build me a mansion in Heaven near You, and save me from Pharaoh and his doings, and save me from the wrongdoing folk.*'"[2]

Asiya was the wife of the Pharaoh who reigned during the Prophet Moses's time. She became Moses's adoptive mother after finding him floating on the Nile river in what we now call a 'Moses basket'. She brought him to her palace, took him under her wing and raised him as her own son. She described Moses to her husband as,

> "A joy to the eyes he will be for me and for your.[3]"

1. Source: Sunan Nasai, Musnad Ahmad

2. Prohibition, *Surah at-Tahrim* (66:11)

3. The Story, *Surah al-Qasas* (28:9)

Isn't that a lovely way to express how we feel about our loved ones? She was the first to believe in him as a Prophet and to subscribe to his message, and she had to endure her husband's torture for being a worshipper of the one unique God.

Hajar – the mother of Prophet Ismail (Ishmael)

Hajar, also known as Hagar in Biblical texts, is mentioned as far back as the Old Testament – that's how exemplary she is to women of all monotheistic faiths. She was the second wife of Prophet Abraham, whose name means 'the Father of many nations'.

Fun fact: The Prophet Muhammad is her direct descendant through her son Ishmael's lineage, so she also holds a very special place in Islam.

When Abraham's first wife, Sarah, realised she was too old to produce an heir, she asked her husband to marry Hajar. This was an age-old custom, and sure enough, Hajar bore Ishmael. Later, God miraculously granted Sarah's wish to have a prophetic son, despite her old age, whose name would be Isaac (*Ishaq*).

Abraham has his own dedicated chapter in the Quran, and some of the supplications he made to God are quoted and still recited today: "All praise is due to God who has given me, in my old age, Ishmael and Isaac. Surely my Lord hears all prayers. My Lord, cause me and [some of] my offspring to establish regular prayers. My Lord, accept my prayer. Our Lord, grant Your forgiveness to me and my parents, and all the believers on the Day when the reckoning will come to pass".[1]

God ordered Abraham to take Hajar and their son Ishmael from Palestine to Makkah. Distressed, Abraham submitted to His command and test, while Hajar felt confident that God would look after them. As Abraham was told to do, he

1. Ibrahim (14:39-41)

left them in a deserted valley in Makkah, to where he would eventually return to build the Kaaba with his son Ishmael. When she realised that her husband was following God's orders, she said, "Then He will not neglect us." Her faith was unshakeable!

The mother and her child quickly ran out of provisions on their own. Out of despair, as her son started rolling on the ground out of thirst, she tried to look for help, going back and forth between two hilltops (Safa and Marwa), half a kilometre apart. After her seventh journey, a source of water sprung from the earth by the foot of her baby. At last she was able to suckle him, as he was not yet weaned. The miraculous source of water still flows today and the well has since provided for millions of pilgrims throughout the centuries: it is called zamzam. Zamzam water has many virtues and is said to be blessed – a food that nourishes.[2]

To honour Hajar's journey, Muslims perform a unique ritual as part of the pilgrimage to Makkah. This ritual is called '*Saee*'. We commemorate Hajar's struggle as a mother and admire her strong faith in God as we reenact her frantic race to provide for her baby. Her story also reminds us of how precious water is to humankind, and of the important role that women have played in Islam and society.

The first time I ever performed my *umrah* pilgrimage, I was six months pregnant and so this ritual was very meaningful to me. I loved being able to relate to a woman who was a new mother, and it prepared me for the selfless sacrifices that, like any mother, I would have to make for my children in order to provide what is best for them. Hajar's tireless strength, her hope, her motivation was an inspiration to me. Although my back was aching from the exertion, I was determined to walk in her footsteps – even if it meant taking a ten-minute rest and snacks at each hilltop! I was drinking water from the zamzam well and couldn't believe the energy pulsing through me.

2. Hadith source: Muslim

The next day, we returned for a second time, even though my husband now had to push me in a wheelchair! (In the sacred mosque, wheelchairs are available for everyone to accommodate each individual's needs.) It was such a beautiful, bonding experience for us as a married couple and parents-to-be. At the bottom of the slope, he would run just as Hajar did, and his efforts, patience and support comforted me. A year later, we returned with our six-month-old daughter and the experience was just as meaningful! As my baby nestled in the carrier in front of me, I have fond memories of giving her sips of the precious zamzam water while nursing her.

Mary – the mother of Prophet Jesus (Issa)

The Virgin Mary, known as Maryam to Muslims, is the only woman to have an entire chapter named after her in the Quran. This privilege has been granted to very few human beings – aside from her, only the Prophets Jonah (*Yunus*), Hud, Joseph (*Yusuf*), Abraham (*Ibrahim*), Muhammad and Noah (*Nuh*) have this honour.

The Quranic revelations shed light on the birth of the Prophet Jesus, and on the miracles that started from the cradle – Jesus started to speak as a baby – and continued throughout his life, confirming that he cured blindness and leprosy. Jesus is quoted in his mother's chapter as saying: "I am a servant of God. He has revealed to me revelations and made me a prophet, and made me blessed wherever I may be. He has enjoined on me prayers and charity, as long as I live. He has made me kind to my mother, not haughty or bereft of grace. Peace was on me on the day when I was born, and [will be on me] on the day of my death, and on the day when I shall be raised to life again."[1]

The Quran confirms that Jesus will be resurrected, but denies the fact that he was crucified.

God also condemns the enemies of all Prophets throughout history, and those who hurt the reputation of Mary. In the chapter 'Women' (*An-nisa*), God addresses these people in the following verses: "...and for their disbelief and their monstrous calumny they utter against Mary, and their boast: '*We have killed the Christ Jesus, son of Mary, God's Messenger.*' They did not kill him, and neither did they crucify him, but it only seemed to them [as if it had been] so. Those who hold conflicting views about him are indeed confused, having no real knowledge about it, and following mere conjecture. For, of a certainty, they did not kill him."[2]

1. Mary, *Surah Maryam* (19:30-33)

2. Women, *Surah An-Nisa* (4:156-157)

God always protected His Messengers from enduring torturous deaths inflicted on them by their enemies. For example, Abraham was saved from burning in a fire, as mentioned in the Quran: "But We said: '*Fire, be cool to Abraham, and a source of inner peace [for him]*'".[1]

Fatima – the daughter of Prophet Muhammad

The Prophet Muhammad said that Fatima will be the leader of the women in Paradise[2] and that he could smell the fragrance of Paradise on her.[3]

Aisha narrated in a *hadith* that she never saw anyone more devoted to the truth than Fatima, and added, "She bore remarkable resemblance to Allah's Messenger: her way of speaking, sitting, standing and walking – in other words all her manners and gestures were exactly like his. She earned the nickname '*Az-zahra'* – the splendid and radiant one, as she was known for her honesty, piety and steadfastness."

Fatima was Muhammad's youngest daughter and was born before he had been given his prophethood. She stood by him even when everyone else abandoned him and provided him with comfort. When her mother Khadija passed away, she was the one that took her mother's place and cooked for the Prophet.

In the early days of Islam, the Prophet was praying in front of the Kaaba when a few men began to plot against him behind his back. One of them took the guts of a camel and, to humiliate the Prophet, dumped the filth on his back while he was praying. Fatima, not even a teenager when she witnessed this, immediately came to help him, wiping off the dirt with tears in her eyes. The Prophet said to her, "Do not cry my daughter; Allah will help your father and will give him victory."[4]

1. The Prophets, *Surah Al-Anbya* (21:69)

2. Hadith source: Bukhari

3. Source: *Yanabi' Al-Mawadda*

4. Hadith source: Bukhari

Beyond being an exemplary and loving daughter, she aided the injured at times of war, helping to stop the bleeding and bandage wounds.

She was also the mother of two boys, Hasan and Husain, the only grandsons of the Prophet. They died at a young age and became, in the words of Mohammad, the leaders of the youth in Paradise.

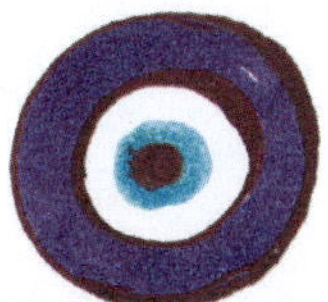

Is there a link with the 'Hand of Fatima'?

No. The popular design can be seen on wall ornaments and apparel and is worn as jewellery.

It is also commonly known as *Hamsa*, or *Khamsa* (meaning 'five', in a reference to the fingers), or the 'Hand of Miriam', in a variety of cultures. Today, the talisman is popular in North Africa and the Middle East, although it can be traced back to representations of goddesses in countless ancient civilisations, thought to boost fertility and protect against dangers. Today it is thought to ward off the 'evil eye' and to be a protective amulet, which is wrong.

Although Islam acknowledges the power of the evil eye and offers invocations to protect against it, it is important to note that Islam does not support superstition, charms, or amulets of any kind.

Nothing can protect us but God; our most powerful tool to ward off evil is prayer and invocation to Him alone.

4. THE MANY FACETS OF MUSLIM WOMEN TODAY

While we can look up to the most pious women in history or admire the inventive minds of the Golden Age, fabulous women are all around us right now. Muslim women can't be defined by the scarf on their head or by the mainstream media stereotypes. You'll find that many values are compatible with Islam.

Christine: Muslim and artist

"

A picture is worth a thousand words. The saying couldn't be truer – much like our faith, art leaves room for imagination and invites hope in our hearts.

My colours allow me to highlight the beauty of this world and express my emotions. A blank canvas represents a breath of fresh air. When I put it up on my easel in the sunlight, it becomes a white window of endless possibilities in which the story unfolds with each stroke of my brush.

It allows me to look at God's creations with an admiring eye, to notice things I might not otherwise, like the different shades of blues in the ocean... I always admired mosques and Islamic arts, even before I converted to Islam. I've painted many throughout the years and they remind me of my travels.

Art makes me contemplate one of His names: *Al-Musawwir*, meaning The Fashioner, The Shaper, The Designer – of beauty and all things, hidden and unhidden to us. ”

Samira: Muslim and feminist

“

Understanding the feminine side of Islam requires us to understand the role played by women since the time of the Prophet Muhammad. Muslim civilisation would not have been able to reach its highest potential without the contribution of women who were inspired by religious texts to excel in all fields. As the famous saying goes, "Behind every great man is a strong woman."

The first teaching of Islam is to read. The first Muslim women united against ignorance by seeking knowledge for themselves. The Prophet Muhammad did not cease to valorise them and they filled history with wonders.

Unfortunately, even in our era, women are sometimes deprived of their basic rights. That's why Aisha, the wife of the Prophet Muhammad, is such an inspirational woman. She invested all her energy into establishing the truth in favour of women, to the point of rectifying a number of important *hadiths*.

In my *halaqas*, I have spent more than twenty-five years teaching women that 'Islam for women' means benefiting from its rights while assuming our religious obligations to live our spirituality. I encourage all women to be active and contribute to society just as the great Muslim women figures of our past did. They continue to inspire us. ”

Lila: Muslim and minimalist

Minimalism is a growing trend, flowing in the opposite direction to the over-consumption and hyper-connectivity of today's society. Everyone has their own definition of minimalism: a lifestyle; an art of living; a new way of seeing the world. New way of seeing the world? Nevertheless, the fundamental basis of minimalism is to liberate oneself from the superficial, to focus on the essential and to keep only the necessities.

Eight years ago, I arrived in the United Arab Emirates with two suitcases and my fifteen-month old daughter. We had emptied our two-bedroom apartment at home and sold or gave away everything we owned. I realised then that we could live with very little so long as we were together as a family. None of our possessions were missed – absolutely none.

A few years and two more children later, the real turning point came during a family trip to Jordan. Our stay in the desert of Wadi Rum, amidst the down-to-earth simplicity and humility of the Bedouin way of life, was a revelation. This was what we wanted, what we really were.

My husband and I realised that our way of living needed to change. We needed to move toward greater simplicity, more humility, more knowledge and a higher personal and spiritual elevation. We decided to live a life that was less superficial and more in line with who we were: travellers on earth.

When we returned, we sorted what to sell, give away or toss. We worked like ants, piece by piece, object after object, asking ourselves: do we really need this? Is it beneficial to us? Gradually we filtered out everything unnecessary from our home. We decided to live on the ground, as our Prophets did, and replaced our couch with a *majlis* and our bed with a Japanese futon. The TV was replaced by a library of books and games for the kids. We also reassessed our purchasing, making sure to question the necessity of every item we bought.

We have lived this way for a year and a half now and our quality of life has hugely improved. We share precious moments with our children – reading, playing games, or praying and reading the Quran together. Hosting guests is a pleasure: we feel more conviviality and sincerity among our friends. Beyond the material aspect, we have applied the concept to our social lives: which of our acquaintances and friendships bring us good and elevate us closer to God? The further we evolve in this way, the closer we feel to God and to our beloved Prophet Muhammad. After all, wasn't he one of the most ascetic men that ever lived? The essence of his message was an invitation to liberate us from the shackles of this life, to help us focus on the afterlife.

God says in the Quran: "Whatever you have is certain to come to an end, but that which is with God is everlasting. We will certainly grant those who are patient in adversity their reward according to the best that they ever did."[1] Minimalism is a first step toward asceticism, a lifestyle. In the end, it's about authenticity – that's how I would define minimalism. ”

Annah: Muslim and founder of modest fashion line Annah Hariri

“

When I became Muslim, I really had no idea how to dress. I think every girl who becomes Muslim has the same problem – you suddenly think, "What can I wear now?"

1. The Bee, *Surah An-Nahl* (16:96)

For me it was an especially difficult transition because I had always loved fashion and dressing up. Now I struggled to find suitable clothes to fit my lifestyle as both a Muslim and a working woman. I have some friends who converted and immediately started wearing black *abayas* or *burkas*, but that just wasn't right for me. Other women would buy modest undershirts and wear them under everything – from office clothes to cocktail dresses! I didn't like the look of the undershirts and, more to the point, I felt that it should be easier for Muslim women to dress modestly while still feeling comfortable and remaining true to themselves.

So, I started to make my own modest wear. After receiving compliments from both Muslim and non-Muslim friends, I was inspired to launch my clothing line, Annah Hariri. I hope it helps Muslim women today to see that there is a choice when it comes to dressing modestly.

I sometimes have this poem playing during my fashion shows as models walk the runway:

I fell in love.

I fell in love with the *hijab* because I came to understand that, it was not simply a piece of fabric draped over my body to conceal beauty and preserve modesty.

It was a physical manifestation of my submission and connection with my Lord; an external representation of my inner spirituality.

Remember no matter how dark the world gets — be like that star that stands out and shines for others to see.

Muna Jama: Muslim and Miss Universe contestant

I was the first woman to ever wear a kaftan instead of a bikini in the swimsuit round of Miss Universe Great Britain. For me it was all about representation. There were no women like me in such a pageant, and I wanted to make Muslim women feel less alone. My intention was to show them that there could be girls like them on television, on runways, in the modelling industry; that there is a platform for them and an opportunity for them to take part.

It was the right time for it, too, since modest fashion has become so common and has established a place for itself within the fashion industry. Eventually I realised that if no one else was going to do it, it would have to be me!

My message to other women is not to apologise for being yourself. I'm Muslim and I'm British, and I'm extremely proud. Just be open and be honest. The only thing you can do is be yourself – everyone else is taken!

Astri: Muslim and humanitarian

It has been narrated that generosity is a great attribute of God; after all, one of His 99 names is The Most Generous (*Al-Kareem*). Interestingly, if Prophet Muhammad said "I fear upon you wealth, not poverty" it is because he was afraid that we would compete for it – as others have in the past. Islam teaches us that success is not in accumulating wealth, but good deeds.

With that in mind, I've always wanted my career to be a means of helping others. The way I see it, I am donating my time and energy to help refugees in need.

Islam's teachings on charity even apply to our day-to-day lives – we should give preference to the comfort of others over our own, be it a neighbour, a friend or a stranger.

Charity (*zakat*) is one of our five pillars and a means to purify our wealth. Besides, Allah has guaranteed to double our loan unto His credit and multiple it many times. There is really no way you can lose by being generous, whether it's your money, time or efforts! ”

Mayya Al Said: Muslim and Motivational Speaker

“

Coming from the Middle East one would assume that wearing the *hijab* isn't a struggle, but it was – at least in my case. *Hijab* to me is more than just a head covering, it embodies everything that I am today – a Muslim (you don't need to ask what faith I follow it shows!) and it has taught me to stand up for myself since the early age of sixteen.

My mother is French and Christian and my father is Omani and Muslim – at the time, I thought convincing her of my decision was my ultimate test. But to my surprise, she accepted it and supported me with it. The majority rejoiced once they saw me in my new attire and I received lots of hugs and *duas* (supplications). However, there were some who didn't approve, simply because they thought I was too young to make such a commitment and they waited to watch me fail. They are still waiting...

I prayed for His guidance and for the strength to fulfill this part of my religion to the best of my ability. My commitment to God and Islam is one that I never questioned.

I believe the decision to stand up for my right to wear the *hijab* has given me the boost that I needed, which has resulted in being called "inspirational", as I share the challenges in my life with a positive attitude. The world we currently live in needs a lot of love and compassion because – with or without *hijab* – we are in this together.

CHAPTER

4

PRAYER

Remember Me, then,
and I will remember you.

Quran, 2:152

Prayer, in its many shapes and forms, is one of the most important acts of worship in Islam. Its significance is highlighted by the fact that it is the second pillar of Islam, after the testimony of faith.

There's no denying the emphasis God and the Prophet have put on prayer. This is not only because it strengthens our faith and is a way for us to communicate directly with God, but also because it makes us closer to Him, helps to keep us on the straight path, at peace, and cleanses us of our sins. As the renowned Sufi poet and philosopher Rumi once said, "Prayer clears the mist and brings back peace to the soul".

It is said that the angels send blessings to the praying person, record their prayer and ask God for their pardon.

This is how important prayer, known as *salah* in Arabic, is in Islam. The Quran further mentions its significance numerous times, just one example being the verse, "*Indeed, I alone am God; there is no deity other than Me. So, worship Me alone, and establish regular prayer to celebrate My praise.*"[1]

1. Ta-ha (20:14)

The opening of the Quran is both a chapter and invocation, known as *Al Fatihah*, whose verses we recite in every *salah*. If you're at a point in your journey where you feel ready to pray, then this chapter is for you – here is the first one you should learn by heart.

بِسْمِ اللّهِ الرَّحْمَـنِ الرَّحِيمِ
الْحَمْدُ للّهِ رَبِّ الْعَالَمِينَ
الرَّحْمـنِ الرَّحِيمِ
مَـالِكِ يَوْمِ الدِّينِ
إِيَّاكَ نَعْبُدُ وإِيَّاكَ نَسْتَعِينُ
اهدِنَــــا الصِّرَاطَ المُستَقِيمَ
صِرَاطَ الَّذِينَ أَنعَمتَ عَلَيهِمْ غَيرِ المَغضُوبِ عَلَيهِمْ وَلاَ الضَّالِّينَ

Bismillah ar-Rahman ar-Raheem
Alhamdu lillaahi rabbil ‘alameen
Ar-Rahman Ar-Raheem
Maaliki yawmid-deen
Iyyaaka na’abudu wa iyyaaka nasta’een
Ihdinas siraat al-mustaqeem
Siraat altheena an’amta ‘alaihim
Ghairil-maghdoobi alayhim wa ladaalleen
(Ameen)

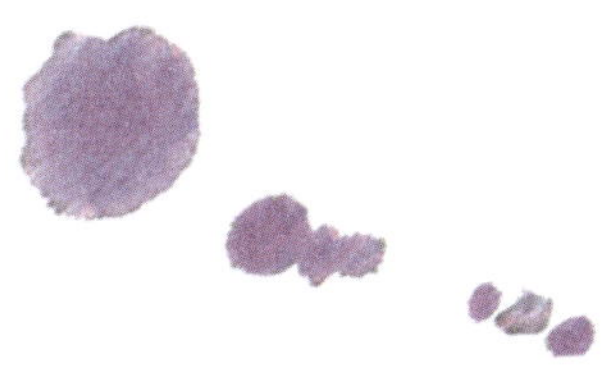

In the name of God, the Lord of Grace, the Ever-Merciful

Praise be to God, Lord of all the worlds,
The Lord of Grace, the Ever-Merciful,
Master of the Day of Judgement.
You alone do we worship and to
You alone do we turn for help.
Guide us on the straight path,
The path of those on whom You have bestowed Your favours,
not those who have incurred Your wrath,
nor those who have gone astray.

(Amen)

For Muslims, prayer represents a window of opportunity during the day and night to connect with our Creator. He has prescribed for us set meeting hours to talk to Him, confide in Him, and it's up to us whether we RSVP or not. This rendezvous strengthens our relationship with God, deepens our spirituality, and holds many rewards. One of God's 99 names is 'The Responder to Prayer' (*Al-Mujib*), because all invocations are answered one way or another, no matter the obstacles we may be facing and even if we think our prayers are being ignored.

Picture this: at any given time, from all corners of the world, thousands of Muslims are praying toward the same direction – how powerful is that? Through prayer, God has united us despite our different backgrounds, languages and cultures, creating a harmony as we all utter Quran's verses in Arabic during our *salah*.

We make a mark on the earth by leaving behind our unique fingerprints as we prostrate in unison, weaving into a larger-than-life synergy.

Focus and humility are key factors in saying our prayers and it is important to try and clear our minds and remove ourselves from distraction in order to concentrate. Rumi also added, "No prayer is complete without presence."

And it's not only spiritually beneficial but also therapeutic – being in a meditative state is known to boost feel-good endorphins and the physical benefits are immense, too, as explained in the chapter 'A Way of Life'.

1. THE SWEETNESS OF FAITH

As you probably know, there are five mandatory prayers in Islam. Their timings vary from day to day, according to solar times, usually by a minute or so.

Fajr	At the approach of dawn.
Dhuhr	When the sun begins to decline after reaching its highest point in the sky.
Asr	When the shadow of any object stretches to 1.5 times its original length.
Maghrib	At sunset.
Isha	The time at which darkness falls and there is no scattered light in the sky.

The five prayers come at prescribed times and we should do everything we can to pray on time, or within the window of time in which each prayer can be performed. If it's an absolute necessity – say you're in a meeting that you can't be excused from or in a class – it's okay to offer a prayer when you're available. Prayers do not have to be performed the exact minute the prayer time starts.

If, for whatever reason, you are unable to pray at all within the window, you should make it up afterwards, as soon as you get the chance. These prayers are compulsory and should not be missed without a valid excuse. Of course, there are concessions given to travellers, pregnant women and the sick, who can pray sitting down, lying down or even just in their hearts, depending on their health condition.

So where on earth do you buy a solar compass? Don't worry, we don't literally go out and measure the shadow of an object when we want to figure out the time for *Asr*! Nowadays the easiest option to be reminded of prayer times is to download an app which will remind you at the beginning of every new prayer time. Your local mosque has a timetable to follow which you can print off from their website and you can even purchase clocks that play the call to prayer at the prescribed times.

Even in today's technology era, it is so easy to get caught up with what we do, especially at work with pressing deadlines and management pressure. If you have a group of like-minded friends, encouraging one another to pray is still the best option, as advised by Prophet Mohammad. I once had a Muslim senior executive at a high-paced company who would kindly remind us to take a short break for prayer time. He was sharp and had a great sense of humour. He would jokingly alternate the call of morning prayer, in which is said, "Prayer is better for you than sleep", by calling out, "*Assalaat Khair minn amal*", which means, "Prayer is better for you than work". Even though he was an executive, he always tried his best to prioritise prayer, which was really inspirational and it encouraged us all to stay on top of our game. Prayer is a key to success: it unlocks our productivity and opens the door of tranquility. Eventually, he earned his title as CPO – Chief Prayer Officer – and the prayer room was packed!

I know it sounds like a lot right now but trust me, once you start praying it will become second nature and you'll look forward to it. Taking the time out of your day won't feel like a burden, it will be a respite; eventually you'll find yourself arranging your day (meetings, appointments, activities) around prayer times and feel uneasy when you're busy at those timings. It's a chance to take a time-out and just reset your spiritual clock.

Once again, I want to point out that we all face different challenges when we start to actively practice Islam. God knows how difficult, or easy, learning verses of the Holy Quran in a new language and the series of movements of the ritual prayer (*salah*) may be for you. He does not expect perfection from us but appreciates our efforts, as we keep trying to incorporate these changes into our life.

While we need to learn verses in Arabic off by heart, it's not about regurgitating words in a monotonous monologue. I find it helpful to understand their meaning in my own language to help me focus, create a connection with God and stay engaged throughout the prayer.

Personally, I like to challenge myself to learn new verses every Ramadan, to keep my prayers diverse throughout the year and switch them up once in a while. If I'm at work I find it useful to know the shorter verses, or if I'm in the mood to enjoy a relaxing and beautiful prayer, I like to recite the more melodious and longer chapters. Prayer is a lifelong pursuit and there is always room for improvement and to make it more enjoyable!

ISRA WAL MIRAJ: WHY WE PRAY FIVE TIMES A DAY

"Limitless in His glory is He who transported His Servant by night from the Sacred Mosque [in Makkah] to the Aqsa Mosque [in Jerusalem] – the environs of which We have blessed – so that We might show him some of Our signs. Indeed, He alone is the One who hears all and sees all."[1]

Learning about *Isra Wal Miraj* was a turning point in helping me to realise the sacred importance of prayer. When I first became Muslim, I started praying gradually; this enticed me to enforce my self-discipline, which helped me build up the number of prayers to reach my desired goal.

1. The Night Journey, *Surah Al-Isra* (17:1)

In the first chapter, we briefly introduced some of the miracles in Islam; this one is mentioned in the Quran as the 'night journey' (*Isra*) that took Prophet Muhammad from Makkah (now part of modern-day Saudi Arabia) to Jerusalem (Palestine) and his 'ascension' (*Miraj*) through the spheres of Heavens and beyond the seventh sky in one night.

Isra Wal Miraj was one of the most significant events that happened during his Prophethood. After his beloved uncle Abu Talib passed away, without his protection the Muslim community faced growing adversity from oppressors in Makkah. That year, the Prophet's beloved wife Khadija also passed away from old age. They had been married for twenty-five years and she was fifteen years his senior. She had been a great support for him, advising him and giving him strength. Khadija is the first Muslim woman, the first follower of the Prophet and is known as 'The Mother of Believers' – not only because she bore the Prophet children but because she was a pillar of the community. Outside, she was a successful businesswoman who did everything she could in her power and wealth, out of good will, to help reverts. At home, she was a source of love and comfort for her husband.

If the loss of two of his most beloved people wasn't enough, during that year, the Prophet also became the target of physical attacks by those who rejected Islam and rejoiced in the death of his uncle and protector. It was during this time that he went to visit Taif, a nearby city, to invite the clans to Islam and was stoned and beaten until he was so drenched in blood that his shoes were clogged to his feet.

This year was an extremely testing and lonely one for the Prophet, so much so that it is known as the 'Year of Sadness,' and it was *Isra Wal Miraj* that helped to lift him out of this suffering, bring him closer to his Creator and bring salvation to Muslims.

It was a journey unlike any other; it was emotional, educational, breath-taking and awe-inspiring, and it was when the Prophet was given instructions for one of the most important forms of worship: prayer (*salah*).

During this miraculous journey the archangel Gabriel and the Prophet ascended the skies and met several Prophets and Messengers. At the first heaven, he found Adam; then Jesus and John the Baptist at the second; then Joseph, son of Jacob at the third; Enoch (*Idris)* at the fourth; then Aaron (Moses' brother) at the fifth; Moses at the sixth and finally Abraham at the seventh. Gabriel guided him through all levels but could not go beyond the seventh sky.

It is when Muhammad continued to ascend on his own that God spoke to him and prescribed prayer to Muslims. At first, He prescribed fifty prayers a day, but when the Prophet returned, Moses advised him to go back to God and ask to decrease the number of prayers. Moses said: "Your followers cannot perform so many prayers. Go back to your Lord and ask for a remission in number." He went back and forth several times, until God reduced the number of prayers to five a day only. Moses once again told him to go back and request fewer, but Muhammad replied: "I feel ashamed now of repeatedly asking my Lord for a decrease. I accept and resign to His Will."[1]

And so, our second pillar of Islam took shape that night. While some in the city mocked the Prophet, his devout followers immediately started the five daily prayers and became even stronger in their beliefs.

Only through prayer have I ever achieved what I personally call 'the sweetness of faith' – a powerful sense of well-being that overcomes your body and leaves your spirit on cloud nine. A heartfelt harmony with my body, mind and soul – and everything that surrounds me.

1. Hadith source: Ibn Al-Qayyim

24/7 HELPLINE TO GOD

In Islam, we believe in a direct communication with God without any intercessor. Although the five daily prayers are the mandatory ones, there are diverse types of spontaneous prayers as well, which we perform when we want to strengthen our connection with God, earn more rewards, ask for forgiveness or just to thank Him. These supererogatory prayers are completely optional and the priority is to first master your five daily prayers, so don't let these overwhelm you.

As a new Muslim, you'll often hear people say, 'Remember me in your *duas*,' or, 'Make *dua* for me.'

A *dua* is an invocation or supplication, a thought that can be said inside your heart and mind only, or out loud if you prefer, and doesn't involve the physical movements on a prayer mat. When people ask you to make *dua* for them, they're simply asking you to remember them in your prayers and to pray for them. The best invocations are the ones made without the person even knowing, as they are the most sincere. Sincere intentions go a long way in Islam!

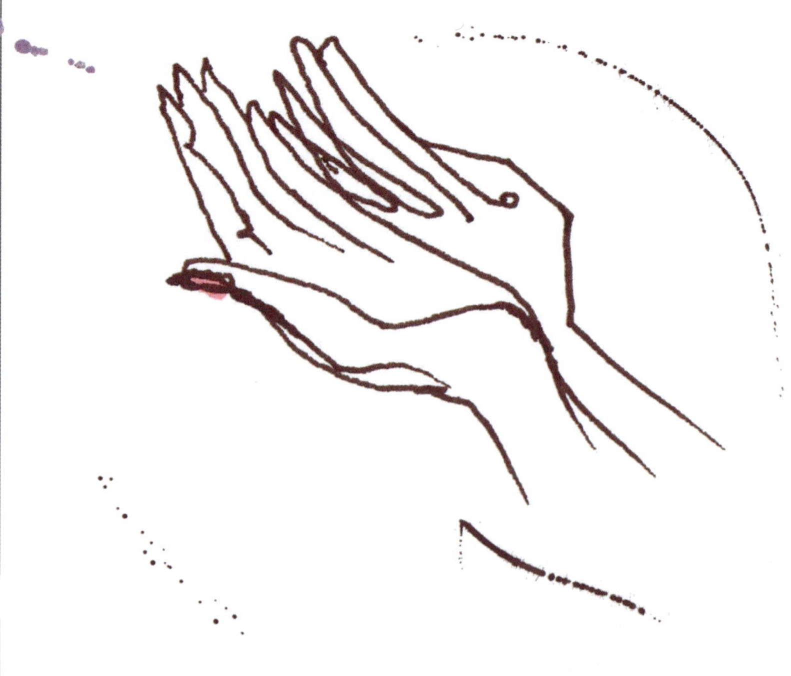

A *dua* can be said any time, any where, in any language, in any physical condition and in any state as it does not require you to preform ablutions. It can also be formulated during the prayer when you put your head down on your prayer mat – this position is called *sujood.* Prostrating is very dear and meaningful to us, it's when we feel the closest to God and contemplate His magnitude – ironically, putting the highest part of our body (our forehead) on the lowest point on earth, is when we say that God is The Most High (in Arabic *Subhaana Rabbi Al-A'laa*, which can be translated to "Glory be to Allah My Lord, the Most High"). When it comes to humbleness and adoration, it doesn't get better than this! We are encouraged to also speak to Allah from the heart in this position and this can be done in any language that we are comfortable in. Additionally, a *dua* can also be said right after prayer as we put our hands up close together.

There is a name of God for any situation in life, so knowing His 99 attributes comes in handy when invoking Him. You can ask 'The Provider', 'The Preventer of Harm', 'The Loving One' anything; talk to Him and thank Him for all the blessings in your life, cry, confide… the list is endless!

Do you want a special recipe to overcome your challenges with ease? Life is a rollercoaster and we all face various situations when we stand at a crossroads and need to make a decision. As we're too involved, it's difficult for us to know what can harm or benefit us. In this situation, we need a little help to choose the right way forward with grace, so we rely on 'The Knower of All'. God says in the Quran: "It may well be that you hate a thing while it is good for you, and it may well be that you love a thing while it is bad for you."[1] To choose the right path, God provided us with one of Islam's gems: the Guidance Prayer, known as *Salat al-istikhara*.

The need for guidance can be anything, from whether or not to marry someone to accepting a new job, and wanting to be content with whatever the outcome is. The Guidance Prayer should be performed as a physical prayer followed by a special invocation. It's an amazing prayer and unique to our faith – I've even recommended this special prayer to non-Muslim friends.

1. The Cow, *Surah Al-Baqarah* (2: 216)

GUIDANCE PRAYER

اللَّهُمَّ إِنِّي أَسْتَخِيرُكَ بِعِلْمِكَ وَأَسْتَقْدِرُكَ بِقُدْرَتِكَ وَأَسْأَلُكَ مِنْ فَضْلِكَ الْعَظِيمِ فَإِنَّكَ تَقْدِرُ وَلَا
أَقْدِرُ وَتَعْلَمُ وَلَا أَعْلَمُ وَأَنْتَ عَلَّامُ الْغُيُوبِ اللَّهُمَّ إِنْ كُنتَ تَعْلَمُ أَنَّ هَذَا الْأَمْرَ خَيْرٌ لِي
فِي دِينِي وَمَعَاشِي وَعَاقِبَةِ أَمْرِي فَاقْدُرْهُ لِي وَيَسِّرْهُ لِي ثُمَّ بَارِكْ لِي فِيهِ وَإِنْ
كُنْتَ تَعْلَمُ أَنَّ هَذَا الْأَمْرَ شَرٌّ لِي فِي دِينِي وَمَعَاشِي وَعَاقِبَةِ أَمْرِي فَاصْرِفْهُ
عَنِّي وَاصْرِفْنِي عَنْهُ وَاقْدُرْ لِي الْخَيْرَ حَيْثُ كَانَ ثُمَّ أَرْضِنِي به

'Allahumma inni astakhiruka bi'ilmika, Wa astaqdiruka bi-qudratika, Wa as'alaka min fadlika al-'azlm Fa-innaka taqdiru Wala aqdiru, Wa ta'lamu Wala a'lamu, Wa anta 'allamu l-ghuyub. Allahumma, in kunta ta'lam anna hadha-l-amra Khairun li fi dini wa ma'ashi wa'aqibati amri (or 'ajili amri wa'ajilihi) Faqdirhu wa yas-sirhu li thumma barik li Fihi, Wa in kunta ta'lamu anna hadha-lamra shar-run li fi dini wa ma'ashi wa'aqibati amri (or fi'ajili amri wa ajilihi) Fasrifhu anni was-rifni anhu. Waqdir li al-khaira haithu kana Thumma ardini bihi.'

It is indeed in the remembrance of God that people's hearts find their comfort.[1]

1. Thunder, *Surah Ar-Ra'd* (13:28)

2. Hadith source: Sahih Al Bukhari

O Allah, I seek the counsel of Your knowledge and I seek the help of Your Infinite Power, and I beseech You for Your Great Bounty. Surely, You are Capable and I am not. You know and I know not, and You are the Knower of the unseen. O Allah, if You know that this matter (mention it here) is good for me in my religion, in this life and the afterlife — then ordain it for me and make it easy for me, then bless me in it. And if You know that this matter (mention it here) is bad for me in my religion and in this life and the afterlife — then distance me from it, and ordain for me what is good wherever it may be, and help me to be content with it.[2]

Besides the Guidance Prayer, there are other formulated invocations for almost everything in your daily routine – from waking up to going to sleep, including travelling, protection from the evil eye, forgiveness and more. Nowadays, many apps or books provide a guide to all the existing *duas*. A good comprehensive one is 'Fortress of a Muslim' – it has the invocations in English, Arabic and the transliteration, which is great for those who can't read Arabic.

Remembering God is considered another form of devotion, which we call *dhikr*, literally meaning 'to remember'. It involves repeating certain phrases to remember God, such as *Al-hamdulillah*, which means 'Praise Be to Allah', or *SubhanAllah*, meaning 'Glory Be to Allah'. The purpose of *dhikr* is to become closer to Him by remembering and pondering on the meaning of the phrases.

You may have noticed people holding prayer beads or special clickers (called *tasbeeh*). These are used to count the number of salutations, similar to rosary beads in Christianity. We can also use our fingers to count and, in the time of Prophet Mohammad, people would also use date stones. The concept may seem quite abstract but when you remember God in a quiet place and you really focus on your connection with Him, your meditative state will soothe your heart and enlighten your spirit.

2. ABLUTIONS? ENLIGHTEN ME

> Believers, when you are about to pray, **wash your faces, and your hands and arms up to the elbows,** and pass your wet hands lightly over your heads, and wash your **feet up to the ankles.**[1]

While invocations can be recited whenever and wherever, performing ritual prayers requires certain preparations. Praying is a spiritual and special moment where we come before God and communicate with Him. It is only respectful that we do so in a clean and tidy manner. Imagine you have an appointment with the Queen of the United Kingdom – you wouldn't show up in an unkempt state with stained clothes or worse, would you? Likewise, when it's time to pray not only should our bodies be clean but our clothes should be clean and tidy as well. So to get ready, first we perform ablutions (*wudhu*), a cleanliness ritual performed before prayer, put on clean clothes and pray in a clean place. Cleanliness, you'll find, plays a really important role in Islam.

1. The Repast, *Surah Al-Ma'idah* (5:6)

It is related in a narration that "when a person makes ablutions and washes his or her face, all those sins committed with the eyes are washed off with the water or the last drop of water. When she washes her hands, all those sins which she had committed with her hands are washed off with the water or the last drop of water. When she washes her feet, all those sins which she had committed with her feet are washed off, until she is completely purified from all sins."[1] Here, the narrator refers to minor sins obviously, such as cursing, etc.

There are major ablutions too, which consist of full body washing, called *ghusl*. This is done whilst bathing and after the completion of your period or after every sexual relation with your husband. Prayers can't be performed until the body is in a state of cleanness.

Here are a few tips I have learned, which can also help you get started in your research and performing ablutions:

- There are countless books and videos online on how to perform ablutions. I personally had a print-out which I laminated and kept close to my sink until I remembered how to do it on my own.
- If you need to relieve yourself, do that first before starting your ablutions to avoid distraction while you're praying.
- Always rinse your private parts after using the toilet – keep a bottle of water beside it and refill it, use the bassinet, or you could install a hose.
- Be mindful of using as little water as possible.
- You can make it a habit to make your ablution while you're showering.
- Keep a hair tie handy to make sure that fixing your hair does not distract you during ablution and prayer.
- If you haven't taken off your socks or stockings since your last ablution, you can keep them on – instead of washing your feet, then you can simply wipe the top of each foot once with a wet hand and voilà!

1. Hadith source: Muslim

- One *wudhu* is considered valid until it is broken – going to the toilet (urine and stool), passing wind, sexual relations, vomiting, falling asleep, bleeding and fainting are things that invalidate your ablution.
- During prayer, if you suddenly need to go to the bathroom and can't hold it, then break your prayer, relieve yourself and repeat both the ablutions and prayer. If you've recently delivered a baby, you'll know exactly where I'm coming from!

As with everything else, note that there exist areas of differences from one school of thought to another. It is worth spending a little time researching and talking to someone you trust in order to get the basic requirements for ablutions. It can be really fun to ask a friend to teach you, too!

Ablutions – check! Now make sure your clothes are clean and that your hair and body are covered with loose, opaque clothing. There are prayer clothes that are quick and easy to put on and take off – I highly recommend those.

Then, roll out your prayer mat towards the *qiblah* – did you know that all Muslims across the world stand facing the same direction towards the Kaaba in Makkah (known as facing the *qiblah*)? Again, you can easily download any free app on your phone to know which direction to face. The old-school method requires a compass; look up the coordinates for your city online to help you set it up. If you buy a compass in an Islamic store, there should be a booklet with all the global coordinates.

Choose a clean place to pray. A prayer mat is great, although not essential – some women just lay down their coat, scarf or beach towel and pray on top of it. However, a mat does help to define your meditation space and for this reason it has become a symbol of prayer. Besides, it's easy to wash and keep clean.

When you're outside, finding a clean place to pray might be difficult, especially if you're in a public place. As a last resort, changing rooms in clothing stores are a good place to pray when you're out for a long time, as they're private. Avoid dirty places like bathrooms and, if you're travelling, be mindful of local laws prohibiting acts of worship outdoors. Throughout my Islamic journey, I've prayed in loads of random places – museums, ice-rinks, on the beach, and even at a theme park!

HOW TO FOCUS:

Prayer should be a time of meditation, reflection and relaxation. Therefore, it is important to stay focused and to remove yourself from distraction. We should not even speak to others when we are engaged in prayer.

So, turn the TV off and put your phone on silent mode because you're about to have a unique connection with your Creator. Here are a few tips – feel free to write your own thoughts in the margins on the side.

- Do not look around; try to find a focus point on the floor in front of you.
- If you have children you can keep them close to you. Make sure they are in a safe environment so you won't worry.
- If you're pregnant or ill, you can pray on a chair or in a sitting position.
- When your head is on the floor, it should be between both hands and the fingers should be together pointing towards Makkah. The stomach should be close to the thighs and the arms close to the sides. (It is important to note that this slightly differs for men, who keep their stomach away from their thighs and arms away from their sides).
- You can keep your prayer mat clean by folding it inwards so the inside is protected and doesn't get dirty when you put it away. For a bit of aromatherapy pleasure, I like to

throw in blooms, like jasmine flowers or dried lavender, and let their essential oils release when I unfold it at the next prayer.

Prayer Kit Essentials:

- A compass or a *qiblah* app on your phone
- A clean prayer mat
- A clean prayer outfit
- A clean pair of socks
- Prayer beads or a clicker

When buying beautiful prayer mats or beads, check your intention! As pretty as they can be, remember that they're supposed to be used for worship, not as ornaments.

When you first start learning how to pray, it can be overwhelming. There are loads of books on how to go through the actions and it's okay to keep them in front of you when you're first learning, to help you go through the sequence of motions. Once you go through it a few times, you'll realise that these are repetitive cycles (each cycle is called *raka*) – it's really not difficult!

ON YOUR PERIOD? "I'M ON HOLIDAY"

Ah, that time of the month. Cramps, swelling, bleeding, excruciating pain. During this time, God has exempted us from praying for our comfort and hygienic reasons (because blood nullifies ablution and so we're not clean when we're menstruating).

Once our cycle is over, we have to take a mandatory bath before we can pray again (*ghusl*). Prayer is mandatory for every Muslim; however, this is one of two occasions in a woman's life when she is 'on holiday'. The other applies to post-natal bleeding. In this case, the grace period lasts up to forty days, after which we should take a bath and start praying again, even if we're still bleeding.

While we have to make up the fasts we miss when on our periods during the Holy month of Ramadan, we don't have to make up any of the prayers missed in these two cases.

You might hear people being a bit extreme and saying you can or can't do x, y and z when you're on your period. Don't overcomplicate things! Aisha, the wife of the Prophet, narrated a situation where her husband Muhammad asked her to pass his prayer mat to him. When she pointed out that she was menstruating, he said, "Your menstruation is not in your hands!"[1] She further narrated that he would lay with his head on her lap and recite verses of the Quran while she was menstruating.[2]

1. Narrated by Aisha
2. Narrated by Aisha

Just remember the below:

- It is fine to read the Quran to study it or teach it.
- Be careful not to touch the Arabic Quran (*Mushaf*) during this time, as God says, "that only the purified can touch"[3] it. By the way, cleanliness also concerns men and, like us, they also cannot touch it unless they have made their major ablution (*ghusl*). This does not apply to a translated copy of the Quran.
- Complete your mandatory bath once your period is over, then you can resume prayers.
- According to some schools of thought, you can enter a mosque so long as the flow is not so heavy that it might leak on the floor and dirty it – the mosque is considered a place of purity and cleanliness.
- You can attend *Eid* prayer without joining in the prayer.

This highlights the importance of cleanliness in Islam. Remember, Islam was revealed in 609 AD, so all forms of ablutions and concern for purity and sanitation were ground-breaking at the time! Even ten centuries later, French King Louis XIV, also known as the Sun King, and the royal family would clean only visible parts such as the face, neck and chest for women, while odours were masked with lavish perfume.

3. The Inevitable Event, *Surah Al-Waqi'ah* (56:79)

3. THE MOSQUE

The mosque has a very special role in Islam. It's not just a place of worship but the hub of the Muslim community, a spiritual retreat and a place of knowledge and guidance. Mosques are places where we can come together to pray, learn and make friends or just relax and meditate.

In fact, I worked for two major real estate developers in the Middle East and it is generally mandatory to include a mosque in every newly designed neighbourhood, as they are such an integral part of a Muslim community.

For Muslim reverts, the mosque can be even more important. Here we can meet other women and reverts just like us, learn more about Islam and interact with the scholars or *imams* to have our questions answered. Many Muslim reverts have also found their spouse through interactions at their local mosque! The community can become a real support system and like a second family. In Islam, this community of people is called the *ummah*.

WHAT DOES A MOSQUE LOOK LIKE?

A traditionally designed mosque, or *masjid* in Arabic, consists of a main building, at least one dome and at least one minaret. However, the designs vary according to the traditional architecture of the country and region in which the mosque has been built; some are extravagant while others are minimalist. Many prefer to have a simple mosque without much decoration to reflect the simplicity and humbleness of Islam and Muslims. However, grand and beautiful mosques also exist, and their Islamic architecture and history can be a source of pride and inspiration for many of us. Of course, in countries where people are very poor or in need, money should be spent to help them before it is spent on beautifying our places of worship. Some of the aesthetics, like the dome and minaret, are not even required in Islam, even if they do serve a purpose. Some scholars are even opposed to building minarets as the mosques in the time of the Prophet Muhammad didn't have them. In practice, all we really need is space, cleanliness and a carpet.

The dome traditionally helped the *imam* to be heard indoors, as the sound waves would bounce in and out of the dome, making his voice louder. Today, however, the person who leads the prayer usually has a microphone and his voice can be heard through the mosque's audio system.

The minaret is a tall tower attached to the mosque which the *muezzin* would traditionally climb and then recite the call to prayer so that it could be heard from beyond the mosque. The first *muezzin* was Bilal ibn Rabah. He was born into a life of slavery (his mother was an Abyssinian slave and his father an Arab slave), however, he rose to become the first *muezzin* and a trusted and loyal companion of the Prophet. Today, there are usually speakers in the minaret so the *muezzin* recites the call to prayer from inside the mosque but it is still heard from outside.

There are three key elements a mosque must have inside its walls: the prayer hall, called the *musallah*, the pulpit from which the imam conducts sermons (the *minbar*), and the *mihrab* – a niche in the wall which indicates the direction of *qiblah* toward the Holy Kaaba in Makkah. They don't have to be fancy as in some mosques but they do have to be there!

You might find prayer halls in places outside of a mosque, like in a mall or airport. In most cases these are just prayer areas without an *imam* or *muezzin*. They're not community hubs, just a simple, clean place to pray when out and about.

Other features inside most mosques include an ablution area: this is more than just a normal washroom, as it has special sinks with seats so you can easily wash your feet; there are separate areas, and separate entrances to the mosque, for men and women. Some mosques have an Islamic centre with a library, classrooms, offices and even halls that can be hired out for events. There may be a noticeboard, so be sure to check if there are any upcoming events or workshops you'd like to attend.

You might notice that, unlike in churches and temples, where there are statues or paintings of saints, idols and deities, there are no pictures or statues inside a mosque. There are various reasons why, the main one being that God is not a person that can be depicted. We don't need visual objects to be able to worship our Creator; we remember Him in every blade of grass and every cloud in the sky. Drawing God and any of the Prophets is hugely disrespectful to Muslims, even more so when satirical.

That's why usually the only indoor decorations will be beautiful Arabic calligraphy of verses from the Quran, chandeliers, colourful mosaic tiles or a beautifully carpeted surface, depending on which country you're in.

The design of mosques in Morocco, for example, differ from the ones in the Gulf to the ones in India or Pakistan and the Far East. That's another beautiful thing about Islam and Muslims: we all hail from different corners of the globe and the architecture of our mosques reflects our unique cultures. In fact, in many non-Muslim continents like America and Europe, mosques don't always look any different from other buildings. Building a mosque from the ground up is expensive, so many communities buy an ex-school, ex-office or even ex-church or ex-pub and turn it into a mosque. That's what's so amazing about Islam – it's the present and future that matters, not the past. Anything or anyone has the potential to change.

Women usually have a dedicated section at the mosque; it is sometimes above the men's section, sometimes behind the men's section or adjacent to it. Within the women's prayer hall, you'll find prayer clothes, Qurans and Islamic books, as well as chairs for the elderly, pregnant women or the less able to use while praying.

I've seen all sorts of different layouts across the world – in the Middle East, I've seen two women's areas in one mosque, one being child-friendly so the noise doesn't cause a distraction for everybody. In North America, I've seen men and women praying in the same room, with a curtain in between or women simply standing behind the men. This was the case back in the day, as narrated by jurist and teacher Fatima bint Qays: "The people were called to prayer, so I rushed with the others to the mosque, and prayed with the Messenger of God. I was in the front row of women, which was just behind the last row of men."[1]

Did you know that all rituals are still performed together today in the Grand Mosque of Makkah in Saudi Arabia, *Masjid al-Haram*? It is the largest in the world, in which the Holy Kaaba is nestled.

1. Hadith source: Muslim

WHO'S WHO IN THE MOSQUE?

In Islam, the *imam* serves as the leader of the Muslim community in the mosque's locality – he is the one who leads the prayers and conducts the sermons, and he is selected at the community level. However, in Islam, the *imam* has no authority over the worshippers of the mosque. He is as equal as every other Muslim and cannot intercede on behalf of anyone.

In Islam we don't talk to God through anyone – we communicate with Him ourselves. The *imam* can perform a marriage ceremony, can lead prayers and is held responsible by God to educate and guide all the worshippers whom he leads in prayer.

A *sheikh* in Islam is different from an *imam*. A *sheikh* is an Islamic scholar who can answer questions on Islamic jurisprudence and can offer advice and guidance. Islamic scholars dedicate their lives to studying Islamic law, theology, the Quran, the life of the Prophets and so on. While a *sheikh* may also be an *imam*, an *imam* cannot be a *sheikh* without the approved Islamic education.

The *muezzin* is in charge of the call to prayer. This is a big responsibility and is usually given to someone who is gifted with a beautiful voice and who is always punctual with his prayers. He can lead the prayer if the *imam* is absent.

A distinctive trait in Islam is that all these men are considered brothers: they are equal and have the same rights. Therefore, *imams*, *sheikhs* and *muezzins* can also marry women and have a family like everyone else. Women can be scholars too – the term *sheikhah* is a term used to describe Muslim women scholars. Women can also be *imams* of congregations of women, such as the female *imams* of China.

Rue Paradis

LET'S GO TO THE *MASJID*!

Commonly referred to as a *masjid* in the Muslim world, the mosque can be a little intimidating at first for some people. I was one of them! Within a few months of converting to Islam, I moved to the French capital, Paris, on my own to go to university. Although I'm originally from France, moving from the quiet city of Muscat, Oman to the hustle and bustle of a large city was a bit of a cultural shock; as well as coming from a Muslim country to a secular one that declared separation of the Church from the State in 1905. As a fresh new Muslim, my first instinct was to immediately visit the famous Grand Mosque of Paris, one of the largest in France, to feel a sense of security and meet other reverts like myself – but I couldn't bring myself to step in! As I recall this, I realise I was making it too much of a big deal. But I felt intimidated and was too conscious of what others thought. I'd think, "I'm white, I don't speak Arabic and I'm not covered." How ironic: at a time when French law was banning Islamic headscarves and other visible religious symbols in state schools, here I was feeling uncomfortable because I wasn't wearing one.

Nowadays I visit local mosques wherever I travel, I meet wonderful people with fascinating cultures and they make me feel like I have a big family waiting to welcome me with open arms wherever I go.

If I returned to Paris, I would not hesitate to walk in without feeling like a tourist. What I didn't realise then is that people don't waste time at the mosque. Worshippers go there with a sincere and modest intention to worship, not to gossip and point out others' mistakes. I would be lying if I said that nobody ever gave me an odd look or made any remarks that made me feel awkward. Is their intention wrong? They probably mean well; as a matter of fact, the Prophet Muhammad encouraged Muslims to give good and sincere advice to worshippers and kindly correcting a mistake in their prayer is even considered to be a duty to all Muslims.

Having said that, my father had an unfortunate experience, and he's not the only one to have felt negatively about visiting a mosque. He felt judged for being non-Arab right as he set foot inside and was unwelcomed by an elderly man who rudely asked what he was doing there. My father is also not the type of person who welcomes brotherly advice trying to guide him as a new Muslim – well-intentioned or not. He has kept away from mosques since, which is tragic as we can find so much peace and solace there.

Sometimes people end up overloading new Muslims with advice that can be overwhelming in the least and off-putting in the worst case. So, remember to be patient with anyone that is giving you advice and give yourself the time you need to build the foundation of your faith, keep learning along this journey.

Remarks must be made tactfully with a gentle approach so that the advice is not offensive and taken badly. Prophet Muhammad had effective methods of dealing with people's mistakes. It is recommended not to exaggerate and to take the person aside to avoid making them feel humiliated in front of others. He never exposed anyone to others by naming them, and remained calm under all circumstances.

Once, a Bedouin entered a mosque in which Prophet Muhammad was sitting with some of his companions. It was narrated that this Bedouin "stood urinating in the mosque. The companions said, 'Stop it! Stop it!' But the Prophet said, 'Do not interrupt him; leave him alone.' So they left him until he had finished urinating, then he called him and said to him, 'In these mosques it is not right to do anything like urinating or defecating; they are only for remembering Allah, praying and reading Quran'. Then he commanded a man who was there to bring a bucket of water and throw it over (the urine) and he did so."[1]

Prophet Muhammad's personality traits were remarkable in so many ways that he serves as an example of behaviour for Muslims today. We should all strive to follow his ways of dealing with people with kindness and patience, so as to avoid causing any hard feelings.

1. Hadith source: Muslim

TO GO OR NOT TO GO?

Whether to pray in congregation at the mosque or in the comfort of your own home is entirely up to you. This is a privilege that has been given to women exclusively, although it is highly recommended to attend the *Eid* prayer in order to be integrated in this important social gathering.

God's intention is not to overwhelm women with five daily obligatory trips to the mosque. So for our convenience, Islam takes into consideration our balance of responsibilities and safety, as well as all the factors that affect the life of a woman – pregnancy, family commitments, living far away, old age, etc.

Back in the day of the revelations, men were told by the Prophet Muhammad not to stop women from going to the mosque, "Although their houses are better for them",[1] he added.

His wife Aisha narrated that when he led the morning prayer *fajr*, "The believing women would pray with him, wrapped up in their outer garments; then they would go back to their homes."[2]

Remember that the doors of the mosque are always open whenever you feel the need to worship there on your own, too.

Kristiane Backer, one of the first presenters on MTV Europe and author of the autobiography 'From MTV to Mecca', describes her uplifting experience praying *fajr* at the mosque in London, shortly after converting to Islam: "Surprisingly, many people turned up at that unearthly hour as if it was the most natural thing to do. Once I managed to get out of bed I actually enjoyed these visits. The quiet of dawn supposedly makes it the best time to pray, because it's a time when a great many angels are believed to be around, carrying our prayers to Heaven. The city was still asleep when we set out, usually a great day would follow such a blessed start. Smiling inwardly, I'd think to myself how, not so long ago, I would have been coming home from a big night out at this time of the morning."[3]

1. Sources: Abu Dawood, Ahmad, Fath Al Baari

2. Hadith source: Bukhari and Muslim

3. Kristiane Backer, From MTV to Mecca - How Islam inspired my life. Page 139

Congregation prayers actually hold many virtues, so it is undeniably important to pray at the mosque. However, we can also benefit from prayer at home, school or elsewhere – in fact we are highly encouraged to do so.

One day, I was having lunch with Muslim women colleagues when I casually started to talk about the five daily prayers. I was explaining how I assumed that, although Muslims knew they were meant to pray five times a day, most must surely settle on an average of two to three daily. Trying to make the point, I asked them all, "How many times a day do you pray?" And they all replied, "Five times, every day!" Needless to say I felt embarrassed to have made that assumption, and I also gave away the fact that I didn't pray as often as I should!

From that day forward, we created a support group and would call each other's extensions or text one another at prayer time to go together as a group. After a while, they nominated me to lead the prayers to make sure that I didn't miss one! This was such a rewarding experience and I learned a few things about how to lead a prayer for a group of women, as per the tradition of Hind (also known as Umm Salama), one of the very first women to convert to Islam and who later married the Prophet.[4]

- To begin, another woman should make the call to prayer in a low voice.
- Stand next to the left of the woman who has called to prayer.
- If you're leading a group, then stand with them in the middle of the first row (not in front of them, as men do).
- During day time, do not recite the verses out loud.
- Once the sun sets, you can recite out loud. If you can't remember the coming line, the woman standing next to you can whisper it to you during prayer.
- Try to keep a set of prayer clothes handy at work, school or in your car.

4. Hadith source: Ibn al-Jawzi

A congregation is when at least two people get together and offer their prayer in such a way that one person leads the prayer. This is irrespective of whether the person is a man, woman or a 'mature' child. If you get married, it is a lovely custom to pray together as a family; this will build love and respect between you and your husband and will create a loving atmosphere for your children and teach them about the importance of prayer in a Muslim home.

MOSQUE ETIQUETTES

In Islam, there isn't anything you absolutely have to do when going to a place of worship, other than wearing modest clothing. There are some etiquettes, however, taken from Prophet Muhammad's life, his wives' and from advice from scholars:

- Wear clean clothes and make sure your body is clean.
- Avoid eating onions or garlic prior to going to the mosque so as not to "offend the Angels" with bad breath.
- Do not wear a strong perfume or incense.
- A mosque is a place of purity where the prayer carpet must be clean, so take your shoes off at the entrance and stack them on the shoe rack. It can get a little messy outside the door as people usually throw them on the floor, so it's good to be tidy and remember where you've put them.
- This is not the place to go wearing shoes with complicated buckles that will take time to remove and put back on. Slippers or flip flops are ideal.
- Enter the mosque with your right foot, saying '*Bismillah*'.
- Put your phone on silent mode (well, the Prophet didn't say that but it's common sense!).
- Don't forget your belongings in the washroom or ablution area! That's a classic.
- It is a custom of the Prophet Muhammad to offer a short prayer upon entering as a greeting and to pay respect to the mosque.

- Greet any sisters you see with greetings of peace: *As-Salaamu alaykum* (may peace be upon you) or in your local language. If they say it first, reply *Wa alaykum as-salaam* (and peace unto you).
- If having private conversations speak quietly and be mindful of other worshippers.
- It's a good idea to bring a clean pair of socks or to make sure you wore a clean pair before leaving your house. It is not obligatory to cover your feet at all, but if you have not had a pedicure in a while, this trick makes many women feel more comfortable.
- Do not cover your face with the full-face veil known as *niqab* during prayer.

Children are welcome inside mosques. You can bring both your young daughter and son with you to the ladies' section or your husband can take them with him. Once they hit puberty, they can stay on their respective side.

The Prophet Muhammad used to shorten his prayer if he heard a child crying, mindful of the mother's feelings. This is how kind and considerate he was. But with small babies, it's important to make sure that their presence won't be a hindrance or nuisance. They could need your attention during prayer so it's not a good idea to bring them to the mosque and let them cry while you pray, thus disturbing others. Of course, if you're witnessing this situation then remember how the Prophet would have dealt with it and do not shout at the mother to look after her child. Raised voices, fighting and cursing are 100% against the etiquettes of the mosque.

THE CALL TO PRAYER

Hearing the call to prayer resonate through the streets of a city is a moving experience for Muslims and non-Muslims alike. Known as the *adhan*, it is recited before every prayer at the mosque.

Hollywood actor Will Smith once said in an interview: "I was in India recently and my hotel was near the Taj Mahal. Five times a day there would be a call for prayer, and it was the most beautiful thing. I was lying in my bed thinking, no matter what your religion is, it would be great to have that reminder five times a day to remember your Lord and Saviour."[1]

It can, and should, also be recited at home during prayer times. You may not know this but the *adhan* is also whispered into the ears of a newborn baby.

1. Newsweek interview 11/27/2008

Allahu Akbar
God is the Greatest.
(said four times)

Ashhadu an la ilahaillAllah
I bear witness that there is no god except the One God (Allah).
(said two times)

Ashaduanna Mohammadur Rasool Allah
I bear witness that Mohammad is the messenger of God.
(said two times)

Hayya 'ala-s-Salah
Hasten to prayer.
(said two times)

Hayya 'ala-l-Falah
Hasten to success.
(said two times)

Allahu Akbar
God is the Greatest.
(said two times)

La ilahaillAllah
There is no god except the One God.

For the pre-dawn *(fajr)* prayer, the following phrase is added here:

As-salatuKhayrun Minan-nawm
Prayer is better than sleep.
(said two times)

Just before the prayer is due to commence, a second call to prayer is recited indoors (called *iqamah*). The only difference between *adhan* and *iqamah* is that '*Qad qamatis salat*' is said twice before the last '*Allahu Akbar*', meaning that the prayer has begun. There is usually a period of five to fifteen minutes between the call to prayer and the start of prayer, giving people enough time to make their way to the mosque.

ALLAHU AKBAR – AND SO THE PRAYER BEGINS

Have you ever seen thousands of people stand at the same time to form perfectly straight rows within a split second? That's the power of the two words *Allahu Akbar* (God is the Greatest). When the prayer begins, you leave all worldly matters behind you and nothing else should matter – be present!

When you stand up for prayer in a straight line there should be no gap between you and the next person – shoulder to shoulder regardless of status, race and age. You could be rubbing shoulders with a princess on your left and a beggar to your right. That's right: we are all equal and sisters in Islam.

You may also pick up a few useful tips below:

- If the prayer has already started, join the rows and catch up on what you missed after the *imam* ends the prayer.
- As long as the *imam* is still reciting the first verses and hasn't bowed yet, your first *raka* (the first cycle of your prayer) is considered complete.
- The *imam* recites verses of the Quran out loud in full for the morning (*Fajr*) and Friday prayers. In the evening and night prayers, he recites the *Maghrib* and *Isha* prayers out loud and the *Dhuhr* and *Asr* prayers in silence.

- A symbol is used in fourteen places in the Quran to indicate when to prostrate before God. Wherever this symbol (illustrated here on the left) appears, on reciting that verse we must kneel and put our head on the ground between our hands in prostration (*sujood* position). This is good to know to avoid being the only person standing when everyone is bowing down! Don't worry, the *imam* will say *Allahu Akbar* out loud to indicate this – do not raise your hands as you would usually, just prostrate directly. This applies to anyone, anywhere, even when only listening to the Quran; but if you're not in a clean state then do it later once you perform your ablutions.

One more thing: do not walk across a person who is praying – it is considered irreverent. Respect for others and their full focus and devotion during prayer is essential. So be mindful of where you pray and anticipate how you're going to get out of the prayer hall if you need to leave in a hurry. Otherwise, be prepared to wait patiently until they finish their prayer.

To make it easier for others to walk about without difficulty while you are praying, pick a quiet spot or simply place your handbag or any object directly in front of you as a sign to allow them to pass through.

4. GET CONNECTED: SPECIAL OCCASIONS

When I think of intense prayer, my mind goes to the Holy Ramadan. During the entire blessed month, and especially in the last ten days, we double our efforts and good deeds in all aspects of life. This means that we spend a lot of our time at the mosque during Ramadan due to the immense rewards and blessings of the holy month. Spending so much time praying, especially at night, makes it an uplifting time of the year and helps to create unique bonds with the other women you meet – although it can be a little physically tiring! But the spiritual experience is immensely rich and uplifting.

The Prophet Muhammad said it is a blessed time of the year. The Holy Quran was revealed in this month, and he also said: "When Ramadan begins, the gates of Paradise are opened, and the gates of Hell are closed, and the devils are chained up."[1]

Did you know that prayer isn't the only thing calculated according to astronomical measures in Islam? The Islamic calendar is the same. Each month of the Islamic calendar starts on the birth of the new lunar cycle and lasts for twenty-nine or thirty days, depending on the visibility of the crescent moon.

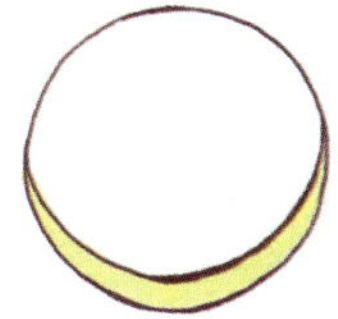

It is for this reason that Muslims must wait to find out what day will mark the start of Ramadan or *Eid*. Traditionally, a new month will only begin with the sighting of the new moon.

There are also special prayers for funerals and there's a unique prayer just for Friday and for *Eid*, too.

1. Hadith source: Bukhari and Muslim

RAMADAN LINGO (YOU'LL HEAR THESE OFTEN):

- *Taraweh* is a prayer performed daily at the mosque straight after the night prayer, *Isha*. This starts the night before the first day of fasting and then takes place all month.
- *Qiyam al layl* is the 'night prayer' that takes place in the middle of the night during the last ten days of Ramadan only, as we seek the 'Night of Decree', known as *Laylat al-Qadr*. God has dedicated a full chapter in the Quran to this very special night:

> From on high have We bestowed it [the Quran] on the Night of Power. Would that you knew what the Night of Power is! The Night of Power is better than a thousand months. On that night the Angels and the Spirit by their Lord's leave descend with all His decrees. That night is peace, till the break of dawn.[1]

- *Itikaf* is a full immersion for a number of days dedicated to prayer at the mosque. You actually sleep and eat there

1. Power, *Surah Al-Qadr* (97:1-5)

while you focus on reading the Quran, learning verses, meditating and praying. Women can choose to do this at home, where they can section a quiet area and retreat for a maximum of ten days.

FRIDAY PRAYERS

According to the Prophet Muhammad, "Friday is the best of days. It was on this day that Adam was created, it was on this day that he was granted entry into Heaven, it was on this day that he was removed from Heaven and the day of resurrection will also take place on this day."[2]

On this day, it is advised to take a full body shower and make your major ablutions before *Dhuhr* prayer.[3] At the mosque, the congregational prayer is preceded by a sermon (the *khutbah*) delivered by the *imam* on various religious aspects like strengthening family ties or giving charity to the needy.

The Prophet also said, "There is such an hour on Friday that if any Muslim makes a supplication in it, it will definitely be accepted."[4]

WHILE TRAVELLING

Travellers are given the option to combine certain prayers and to shorten them. For instance, *Dhuhr* can be grouped with *Asr*, and only half of each prayer is performed. I'm not going to lie, this is very convenient! If you're often on the road or in case you commute from one city to another on a daily basis, it is worth looking this up in books on prayer or speaking to a scholar for a solution that is best suited to your situation.

By the way, on the Day of Judgment, all the spots on which you prayed will testify for you. How amazing is that?

2. Hadith source: Muslim

3. Hadith source: Muslim

4. Hadith source: Bukhari and Muslim

HAPPY EID!

Eid prayers are usually performed in a central location (a *musalla* as described earlier) where the Muslim community from all over the town can gather in a large area rather than in their local mosque (although there are some exceptions). The Prophet Muhammad used to go there on foot by one route and return using a different route. This practice is still carried on today, as well as eating something sweet before the prayer begins, like a date. On his way, he would chant:

"*Allahu Akbar, Allahu Akbar, Laa ilaaha illallahu; Wallahu Akbar, Allahu Akbar, Wa lillahil Hamd.*" (Allah is the greatest, He is the greatest. There is no god except Allah. He is the greatest. All praises and thanks are for Him.)

As you reach the *musalla*, everyone chants this in unison as the festive spirit grows.

The sermon follows a short prayer and takes place early in the morning. Once it is over, women hug and greet each other with '*Eid* Mubarak!' ('Happy *Eid*!') and '*TaqabalAllah wa minkum*!' or 'May Allah accept (this worship) from you and us!' – quite a tongue-twister!

The festivities of *Eid* don't end at the post-dawn *Eid* prayer, though. *Eid* is a joyous time when we dress up in new clothes, give gifts to children and each other, go out and visit friends and family, and, of course, indulge in lots of delicious food.

Once you start your own family, it's important to make *Eid* a special time for children, especially if you're in a non-Muslim country where other religious celebrations like Christmas or Diwali might take precedent. Don't be afraid to create your own family traditions! You can hang up balloons, lights and decorations; bake and decorate cookies and cupcakes together; choose presents for family members together; attend the *Eid* prayers together; and teach kids the importance of giving by donating a little money to charity together.

CHAPTER

5 TOGETHERNESS

"The believer to the believer is like a solid building, one part supporting the other"[1]

Prophet Mohammad

Beyond the Quran and the Islamic way of life, Muslims stand together, united as the *ummah*. The community goes beyond borders: it's not a nation and it doesn't have a homeland. It defies skin colour, handicaps, gender and age and makes us all equal. After all, God says that the Quran was revealed to all of humanity. Everybody is invited.

Its universal concept of oneness defies racism, division and violence. The Prophet Muhammad said: "Do not hate each other, but rather be servants of God as brothers."[2] Together, we can cultivate kindness, acceptance and tolerance and harvest love.

I like to think that women put the *umm* in *ummah*, since it means 'mother' in Arabic. I remember reading the words, "Preserve the women and you'll preserve the nation" (unknown).

The pillars of Islam invite us to play our part in the Muslims' commonwealth by paying charity and helping and supporting one another. They also invite us to regularly interact with our community through random acts of kindness, like visiting the sick or attending a funeral, to bigger community events like weddings, *Eid* celebrations and the pilgrimages *umrah* and *hajj*.

Fairness, justice and dignity are basic Islamic concepts to be distributed without discrimination; a huge responsibility for all of us.

1. Hadith source: Bukhari and Muslim

2. Hadith source: Bukhari

1. SOUL SISTERS

Islam acknowledges our diversity – in our DNA, social status, gender and ethnicity. However, God also points out that we all come from a single soul. We are all children of Adam and, therefore, equal sisters and brothers. That's why you will often hear Muslim women call each other 'sister', and men our 'brothers'. Even a scholar and *imam*, who have more knowledge than us of Islam, are our brothers and sisters in faith. We are all students in our own way, after all.

I didn't expect to meet so many new friends in the community, nor did I anticipate the unique bond I'd feel with other converts like myself. As Dr Seuss says, "We are all a little weird and life's a little weird, and when we find someone whose weirdness is compatible with ours, we join up with them and fall in mutual weirdness and call it love."

Jokes aside, it was truly comforting to find other women who had converted to Islam. I didn't feel that my personality had changed whatsoever after my conversion, but I did feel that people saw me differently. But my fellow converts and I were all in the same boat together – Europeans, Africans, Australians, Americans, Brazilians, ex-Jews, ex-Hindus... We may have come from different backgrounds but we had this amazing thing in common that bound us together: our faith. Under different circumstances, we would probably have never even met each other. But living far from home and away from our families, we celebrated *Eids* together, prayed together during Ramadan and attended classes in the same Islamic centre.

At the centre, we felt accepted and weren't judged according to our nationality or whether we were covered. We were students of Islam on a mission to learn. We encouraged each other's slow but steady progress to better ourselves. I learned that for any woman who makes a prayer for her sister, an angel says, "For you the same".[1]

So, what happened to my non-Muslim friends from before my conversion? Obviously, embracing Islam does not mean cutting off ties of friendship; on the contrary, we can change some of the misconceptions around us. In my case I think that, like many childhood friendships, we grew apart. In the first couple of months as a Muslim, our interests quickly diverged – without noticing it, I completely lost interest in clubbing and drinking. With some people, I had to put some distance to avoid being in bad company and find myself in uncomfortable situations or under peer pressure. To date, I still have childhood friends who respect my beliefs and life choices, as I do theirs, and I am so grateful for their love, friendship and support. Friends also help you stay grounded. With others, the distance didn't help – I have lived in three different countries since converting and after I graduated from high school we were scattered across the world.

Since then, I've made new non-Muslim friends in my adulthood with whom I share a similar interest in religions. We talk about our faiths all the time and it makes me happy to enlighten them about Islam while learning about their religions. The key is to have mutual respect, an open mind and an open heart.

I'm also wary of new friendships with Muslims who push too hard to become more pious, trying to get me 'to the next level' where I may not be ready to go yet. Sometimes, we just have to create distance without letting an unpleasant encounter diminish our experience of Islam.

But overall, one of the many benefits of the sisterhood is that it creates a support system of friendships that bring you good influence, positivity and encouragement. It is said that on Judgement Day we will be gathered with the community we hang out with!

1. Hadith source: Muslim

HOW TO DEAL WITH OTHERS

A general rule of thumb is the following: respect your elders because they have more experience than you and have done more good deeds than you; respect the young as they have committed fewer sins than you! It's like always seeing the glass half full rather than half empty – the brighter side of life.

Of course, it goes without saying that we should keep each other's secrets, not break promises, and not talk behind each other's backs. Talking behind someone's back is considered a major sin; instead, we should always look for the good in others and focus on that.

I was a bit confused when my teacher at my Islamic centre, Markaz Al Salam in Dubai, told me, "I love you for the sake of Allah." What does this mean? What does God have to do with our love for one another? Well, she explained that, in Islam, we believe that God puts love for one another in our hearts.

A narration tells us that on Judgement Day, seven groups of people will be under the shade of the throne of God. Among them will be "two (people) who love each other for the sake of Allah, meeting and parting for that reason alone…"[1]

AVOID THE GREEN-EYED MONSTER & ITS FRIENDS

We've all had those moments – that twinge of envy when a friend gets a brand-new flashy car; that burning rage when someone cuts in front of you while you're driving; that surge of pride in our ego when you accomplish something no one else has…

1. Hadith source: Bukhari

These are all normal sensations and everyone experiences them. So, if you do feel it occasionally, don't beat yourself up over it. However, good character is highly valued in Islam. We are discouraged from being jealous or envious, or losing control of our temper. Instead, we are encouraged to love each other, forgive one another and want for our brothers and sisters what we want for ourselves.

"By the One in Whose Hand is my soul, you will not enter Paradise until you believe, and you will not believe until you love one another. Shall I not tell you of that which will strengthen love between you? Spread (the greeting of) peace amongst yourselves."[2]

To avoid feelings that corrupt the heart and mind, it's important to remember that everything – good and bad – comes from God who says in the Quran: "Such is God's favour which He grants to whom He wills."[3] In other words, there's no point in being jealous of that girl with the fabulous

2. Source: Jaami' al-Tirmidhi

3. The Repast, *Surah al-Ma'idah* (5: 54)

head of luscious locks it's been given to her by God and there's really nothing you can do about it.

Whenever you see something nice that belongs to someone else, say '*Masha Allah'* (God has willed it) and wish the best for them. If you do find yourself getting jealous, recite '*Astaghfirullah'* (I seek forgiveness from Allah). Reciting God's name and remembering Him is said to clean the heart.

"For your Lord had declared: 'If you are grateful, I shall certainly give you more'."[4]

CHECK YOUR INTENTION

Every action depends on its intention. Islam places a huge emphasis on our intentions. Even before we pray or fast, we're required to state our intention to ensure that it's pure.

It's also important for us to check in on our intentions even while we're in the middle of doing something, just to make sure that our intention is still correct. It's really important that every good deed we do is done for God. When everything we do stops being about ourselves or other people and becomes about pleasing God, it's amazing how much happier we become.

Think about it – if you help someone because you want to make them happy, and if they never return the favour or thank you for your help, you'll probably end up feeling a bit resentful at the very least. Harbouring these expectations and ill feelings won't do you any good. But if you do everything for the sake of God, and know that whatever good deeds you do will help you in the hereafter, you'll feel a lot better mentally, emotionally and spiritually.

"Carry out random acts of kindness, with no expectation of reward, safe in the knowledge that one day someone might do the same for you."– Princess Diana.

4. Abraham (14:7)

ISLAMIC CENTRES AND EDUCATIONAL COURSES

Islamic centres are hives of knowledge and information – for Muslims and non-Muslims alike. There is always somebody there available to answer your questions on Islam, and they sometimes organise events with renowned Islamic scholars and speakers, interfaith talks and open-door days.

There are a variety of classes for women of all ages to develop their knowledge and understanding of Islam – from Arabic classes to reciting the Quran or learning about the life of Prophet Muhammad. These are very accessible; usually, Islamic centres offer them free of charge! There are also free online courses, such as with the Islamic Online University.

Tajweed classes: learning the Quran

Muslims are encouraged to learn how to recite the Quran in Arabic, even if it's not their native language. This is because Arabic is the language in which the Quran was originally revealed and we perform our ritual prayers in its original language. *Tajweed* is the specific way of vocalising the words of the Quran – it sounds a little different to everyday Arabic.

In a *tajweed* class, we are taught how to correctly recite the verses in the Quran – everything from Arabic grammar to where to place your tongue and which letters and words to accentuate. All these rules will help you to create a harmonious sound when reading the Quran, even though mastering this art can be a long process. As with acquiring any new skill, patience is essential and not getting discouraged; God sees our efforts and rewards our intention.

Did you know that reciting and memorising the Quran not only cleanses the heart but also helps to keep your mind sharp and protect you from Alzheimer's? In fact, when neuroscientist Mohamed Ghilan researched the reasons for the unparalleled rate of scientific discovery and advancement by Muslims during the Golden Age of Islam, he claimed a link between memorising the Holy Quran and improved thinking.

According to Ghilan, the listening and recitation involved in memorisation stimulates the temporal lobe, which contains the hippocampus – the memory centre of the brain. Likewise, Ghilan explained that the parietal lobes are also heavily engaged during memorisation of the Holy Quran. The left parietal lobe processes reading, writing and speech as well as math and logic problems.

Quranic recitation also strongly activates the frontal lobes and the primary motor cortex of the brain. The frontal lobes deal with higher order functions such as working memory, memory retrieval, speech production, written-word recognition, sustained attention, planning and social behaviour.

Attending talks

Attending a talk or a class, known as *halaqa* or *dars* respectively, is of course beneficial for increasing our knowledge, but it is also said that these circles hold a special blessing for us: "Whenever some people gather in one of God's houses to recite the book of God and study it among themselves – then calmness and tranquility descend upon them, the angels surround them, mercy covers them, and God mentions them to those who are with Him" (the angels).[1]

1. Hadith source: Muslim

COMPLETING THE QURAN

Another lovely and inclusive way in which the community and families unite is for the completion of the Quran. Once you finish reading the Quran from cover to cover, you can make your own invocations and supplications to God. My father-in-law is an *imam* and knows the Quran off by heart in different recitations – it takes him from six to ten days to complete it. At the end of every cycle, he gathers family and friends at home and includes each person in his prayer. It's a really thoughtful way to wish your loved ones well and encourage them in life and it is said that invocations and supplications are accepted upon completing reading the Quran.

I remember when my own father was gravely ill, I asked an *imam* to pray for his speedy recovery with the support of more than one-hundred believers in a congregational prayer. I am sure that their synergy, their positive vibes and their sincere invocations reached God, who accepted their prayers and returned my dad to health.

2. CITIZENS OF THE WORLD

I like to think of myself as a citizen of the world. After much travelling and living in several different countries, I've noticed that only culture and customs change; people are the same. We are all on an emotional journey, we all feel happy and sad, we all look for love and grieve loved ones, and we all feel a need to believe – whether it is in hope, in God, in ourselves, the pattern is the same.

The example of the believers, in their mutual love and mercy for one another is like the example of one body, if one part feels pain, then all of the body suffers in sleeplessness and fever.[1] ”

We can even trace our lineage through generations of DNA to find that, ultimately, we are all a multi-racial mix. I like to think that what differentiates us is our education, our principles and our values. The Quran is a teacher for all mankind, as God says: "You are the best community that has ever been raised for mankind; you enjoin the doing of what is right and forbid what is wrong and you believe in God. Had the People of earlier revelations believed, it would have been for their own good. Few of them are believers, while most of them are evil-doers."[2]

1. Hadith source: Muslim

2. *Al 'Imran* (3:110)

GREETINGS!

Any interaction in Islam begins with wishing peace to one another: *as-salaamu alaikum* means ‘peace be upon you’. The Quran encourages us to reply with an equal or better greeting – so you will often hear in response w*a alaikum as-salaam wa rahmatullahu wa barakatuhu*, meaning ‘may the peace, mercy and blessings of God be with you’.

I have to admit, it’s a really great feeling to be greeted with wishes of peace

THE FIFTH PILLAR – IT’S A WRAP

There’s no doubt that one of the greatest community events on earth is the *hajj* pilgrimage. It brings together more than two million men and women from all over the world every single year! It’s a picture-perfect melting pot of all ethnicities, cultures and ages gathered in the same place at the same time for the same reason.

This fundamental pillar and act of worship can be a once-in-a-lifetime opportunity and is regarded as an invitation from God to His house. It is an expensive trip, so the poor are not obliged to perform it, as well as a physical struggle, hence the sick are exempt. But those with the financial means and good health should not neglect the chance to go.

To show our respect, pilgrims are given a unique title after completing *hajj*: women are called *hajjah*. It’s kind of like calling someone a marathon runner once they have completed their first marathon!

Hajj is the ultimate gathering of Muslims and holds many benefits:

- Walking in the footsteps of Prophets can be an eye-opener and help us strengthen our faith. It helps us visualise the enormity of our religion as it extends open arms to people coming from all corners of the globe. The other pilgrims’ stories are unique, amazing and inspiring – like yours. We utter the same prayers, regardless of our mother tongue, in one single *ummah*. It helps us create ties within the community.

- Furthermore, *hajj* brings us all closer together. We meet people with different educations, cultures, local issues. As we mingle with other sisters in Islam, one's oppression can be felt by another, while another's discrimination is shared. Conversely, one's success story can give others inspiration and motivation. This gathering brings global issues under a single spotlight. It helps us feel united with other Muslims across the world and encourages us to take up their cause as our own. This compassion brings out the best in humanity.
- On the last day, there is a major gathering at Mount Arafat, where Prophet Muhammad delivered his last speech. This stop is a commemoration of his leadership and his accomplishments within the community, and a reminder of how his teachings have reached you across the centuries.
- Last but not least, *hajj* also represents the unified direction and orientation of Muslims – not only do we physically stand together as one nation in a common meeting place, but we hold the same objectives and look forward to a future of unity together.

Have you heard of the great Moroccan traveler Ibn Battuta? In 1325, when he was twenty years old, he set out by camel and donkey to perform *hajj*. The pilgrimage propelled him further into Asia and his travels went on to last 29 years, during which he covered 75,000 miles through North and West Africa to Pakistan, India, the Maldives, Sri Lanka, Southeast Asia and China. At the end of his life, he detailed his journeys in a book called *Rihla* – My Travels. He is less well-known than Marco Polo, although they explored similar places around the same time, but unlike Marco Polo his initial motivation was to connect with God and to perform his pilgrimage while he still had the physical strength and ability to do so. His adventures are worthy of a novel or mini-series on Netflix, too!

I've not met one person who has not grown from the experience of *hajj* – in humbleness, patience and, most importantly, their closeness to God. Ibn Battuta was just one of billions of pilgrims throughout the centuries who made this incredible journey. Human rights activist Malcolm X, also known as Malik El-Shabazz since his conversion to Islam in 1964, is another.

Malcom X's pilgrimage to Makkah proved to be life-altering for him. For the first time, he received an overwhelmingly positive response when he shared his thoughts and beliefs with people from different cultures. When he returned, Malcolm said he had met "blonde-haired, blue-eyed men I could call my brothers". He returned to the United States with a new outlook on integration and a new hope for the future. This time when Malcolm spoke, instead of just preaching to African-Americans, he had a message for all races.

SHADES OF LOVE

In his letter, Malcolm X addresses a major issue that, unfortunately, is still globally relevant today. Racism, colourism and nationalism persist in communities across the world, even though Islam truly encourages not to discriminate against others based on colour or nationality. Beyond colourism, you will find some mosques exclusively for certain nationalities, like North Africans or Asians. In truth, we should all mix together and pray shoulder to shoulder – that's the whole point.

Letter From Mecca (abridged)
Malcolm X, April 1964

Never have I witnessed such sincere hospitality and overwhelming spirit of true brotherhood as is practiced by people of all colors and races here in this Ancient Holy Land, the home of Abraham, Muhammad and all the other Prophets of the Holy Scriptures. For the past week, I have been utterly speechless and spellbound by the graciousness I see displayed all around me by people of all colors.

I have been blessed to visit the Holy City of Mecca. I have made my seven circuits around the Ka'ba, led by a young Mutawaf named Muhammad. I drank water from the well of the Zam Zam. I ran seven times back and forth between the hills of Mt. Al-Safa and Al-Marwah. I have prayed in the ancient city of Mina, and I have prayed on Mt. Arafat.

There were tens of thousands of pilgrims, from all over the world. They were of all colors, from blue-eyed blonds to black-skinned Africans. But we were all participating in the same ritual, displaying a spirit of unity and brotherhood that my experiences in America had led me to believe never could exist between the white and non-white.

You may be shocked by these words coming from me. But on this pilgrimage, what I have seen, and experienced, has forced me to re-arrange much of my thought-patterns previously held, and to toss aside some of my previous conclusions. This was not too difficult for me. Despite my firm convictions, I have always been a man who tries to face facts, and to accept the reality of life as new experience and new knowledge unfolds it. I have always kept an open mind, which is necessary to the flexibility that must go hand-in-hand with every form of intelligent search for truth.

During the past eleven days here in the Muslim world, I have eaten from the same plate, drunk from the same glass, and slept in the same bed (or on the same rug) – while praying to the same God – with fellow Muslims, whose eyes were the bluest of blue, whose hair was the blondest of blond, and whose skin was the whitest of white. And in the words and in the deeds of the 'white' Muslims, I felt the same sincerity that I felt among the black African Muslims of Nigeria, Sudan, and Ghana.

All praise is due to Allah, the Lord of all the Worlds.

Sincerely,
El-Hajj Malik El-Shabazz
(Malcolm X)

God reminds us that it is because of the selfishness of some people and their egos that we are not all united:

Mankind was one single community. Then Allah sent forth Prophets to give them good tidings and warn them; and with them He sent the Book, setting forth the truth, to judge between people over all on which they differed. Yet none other than those who had been given the Book started, out of injustice to one another, to dispute it after clear evidence of the truth had come to them. God, by His will, guided the believers to the Truth, concerning that which they had differed. God guides whom He wills to the straight path.[1]

1. The Cow, *Surah Al-Baqarah* (2:213)

REFUGEES

Human beings should not be deprived of their basic needs – period. Natural resources are a gift from God for our benefit and it is our basic human right to have access to them:

> We have indeed honoured the children of Adam, and borne them over land and sea; and provided for sustenance out of the good things of life; and favoured them far above many of our creation.[2]

2. The Night Journey, *Surah Al-Isra* (17:70)

Bella Hadid, an international supermodel who is half-Palestinian, said in an interview with Harper's Bazaar Arabia that her father, Mohamed Hadid, first came to America as a Palestinian refugee. Explaining that she is proud to be a Muslim, she added: "Thankfully, he was able to come, but it was very hard... It makes me sad that power is getting taken from a lot of people and they're not able to make a new life for their children and their families."

3. LET THE FESTIVITIES BEGIN!

There are two types of *Eid* in the Islamic calendar: *Eid al-Fitr* and *Eid al-Adha*. They bond the community together in many ways: the morning prayer, the hearty food, giving charity and reuniting with family.

Eid al-Fitr marks the end of the Holy month of Ramadan and celebrates our efforts in fasting for a full month. It's a festive period in which we can resume a regular diet and, most importantly, it is a time for sharing. Before the *Eid* prayer it is a duty upon every Muslim family to pay a charity called *Zakat al-fitr* to the poor. It is not necessary to give to the needy in the form of money: the minimum is the equivalent of about 2kg of flour, wheat, barley or rice. This gives them a chance to also enjoy the celebrations.

Eid al-Adha, the 'Sacrifice feast', is the holiest of the two. First and foremost, it commemorates Prophet Abraham's sacrifice.

One night, he had a premonitory dream that he would sacrifice his son. The story is the same across the monotheistic religions, except that in the Quran it is revealed that the son in question is Ishmael (known as *Ismail*). Abraham asked Ishmael to interpret the dream: as he was a devoted follower of God, he told his father that he must obey God's Divine order. But just as Abraham was resigning himself to make the sacrifice, God sent an angel to stop him and gave him a lamb to sacrifice instead.

'The Great Sacrifice' also took place during the *hajj* month (the last month in the Islamic calendar), in which Muslims set out to make the big pilgrimage. On this day, pilgrims perform the *Eid* prayer on Mount Arafat, where the Prophet Muhammad delivered his last sermon before he passed away.

Muslims who can financially afford it usually sacrifice a lamb or goat on this day to eat and share with the poor.

Eid is an Arabic word that is not exclusive to Islam, as it simply means 'festival or holiday' – therefore Christian Arabs wish each other *Eid al-miladal-saeed* at Christmas actually meaning 'happy birthday!' as they celebrate the birth of Jesus. And did you know they also say '*Allah*' for God?

MERRY CHRISTMAS! HAPPY DIWALI!

Muslims are not supposed to celebrate any non-Islamic occasions such as Holi, Hanukah, Valentine's Day, Halloween, New Year's Eve, or birthdays. For born-Muslims, this is a no-brainer, but for converts it's a different ball game. What if your family invites you? It's important to stop for a second and think about the origin of these events and what our intentions are.

For some, it's Holi or Hanukah; in my case, it's Christmas – Santa, gifts under the decorated tree, the street lights, the candy and Mariah Carey's Merry Christmas CD on loop... Although my entire family was atheist in my tender years, we always came together to exchange gifts and to gather around for a big dinner at Christmas. It was the only time in the year when both sides of the family met, with the grand-parents, uncles, aunts and cousins reunited. Us kids were allowed to stay up late, waiting for Santa to leave gifts under the Christmas tree. There was always a jolly family spirit and I have fond memories of each Christmas.

Every year I get asked if I miss Christmas. I don't celebrate it anymore – but I feel like I've had a two-for-one deal as I now get two *Eids* a year! Of course, I can't celebrate *Eid* with my entire family like I used to for Christmas, and it's the family reunion aspect that I miss the most.

I live abroad, so I don't get the opportunity to even spend Christmas with my extended family anymore. However, for many Muslim converts, their family still invites them to celebrate their traditional holidays together – and that's when the awkwardness and questions begin. Do I bring gifts? Can I wish them a Happy Christmas when I don't believe in it?

God says in the Quran: "Do not revile those whom they invoke instead of God, lest they revile God out of spite, and in ignorance. Thus have We made the actions of every community seem goodly to them. Then to their Lord shall they all return, and He will explain to them all that they have been doing."[1]

Picture this: you're invited to your family's Christmas dinner; you have no other plans and your grandparents, parents, aunts, uncles and cousins will be there. There are two options for you: to accept or to decline the invitation. What are you going to do?

This is undeniably a test in our journey – there will be alcohol and non-*halal* meat on the table, which is forbidden to us and might be a temptation; praying might be challenging too; and conversations on religion could be uncomfortable.

Your first option is to go. After all, besides your faith, you haven't changed, have you? Still like chocolate, still laugh at the same jokes! So, this is an opportunity to show your family that you are a balanced woman with an open mind and that you live a happy life. You will receive gifts and show your generosity and appreciation in return. Your light will attract people toward you and you can spread the secret to your new happiness.

1. Cattle, *Surah Al-An'am* (6:108)

Your second option is to decline the invite. This is the beginning of a secluded life – you withdraw from society, shut down your relationships and choose a future of solitude. Imagine how many loved ones you will hurt – your mother and father, who went through so many sleepless nights when you were a baby, who have made endless sacrifices for you; siblings who you grew up and shared meals with. Where is the gratitude, love and respect that Islam teaches us? After all, it is your parents' right to see you and spend time with you. If you refuse, they will conclude that Islam has taken you away from them, brainwashed you and forced you to cut off ties – which is obviously far from the truth. Twenty or thirty years from now you may regret this choice when you need family and friends around you.

You don't need to invent a new you **when you become a Muslim – be yourself!** Keep your good character traits and stay in touch with your loved ones who have made you who you are today. **That's Islam.**

So, you like the first option but you're scared of your parents and close ones making hurtful remarks about Islam and God's messengers? Check this out – the Prophet Muhammad's sister-in-law, Asma, once received a visit from her mother, who was not a Muslim. She was not sure whether she could host a non-Muslim, even a relative, and accept her gifts. Through her sister Aisha she asked advice from the Prophet. He replied that she should both welcome her mother into her house and also accept her kind gifts. On this occasion, the following verse of the Quran was revealed to Him: "God does not forbid you to deal kindly and with full equity with those who do not fight you on account of your faith, nor drive you out of your homes. God loves those who behave equitably. God only forbids you to turn in friendship towards those who fight against you because of your faith, and drive you out from your homes, and help others to drive you out. Those of you who turn towards them in friendship are indeed wrongdoers."[2]

So, keeping strong family ties is paramount, but what about exchanging gifts and wishes with non-Muslim friends and colleagues? Scholars argue that our worship for Allah alone takes precedent and that we must be mindful of this. Therefore, they do not judge it appropriate to take part in other religious celebrations. However, we are striving for multi-cultural coexistence and tolerance, so we should always respect each other's choices. As God said in the chapter of the Quran called 'The Disbelievers', "You have your own religion and I have mine."

2. Women Tested *Surah al-Mumtahanah,* (60: 8-9)

4. DEATH

"And He is the One Who originated you all from a single soul, then assigned you a place to live and another to be laid to rest. We have already made the signs clear for people who comprehend."[1]

Of course, death is an inextricable part of life. It hurts most when it takes our loved ones away. The Islamic scholar Mufti Ismail Menk instructed, "Always leave loved ones with loving words. It may be the last time you see them."

As I've mentioned before, I learnt about death at a young age, when my older brother Stéphane passed away, a few days before his sixteenth birthday. At the age of ten, I realised that life hangs by a thread and that today could be our last day.

I remember attending my brother's funeral like it was yesterday – it felt as though our lives had been turned upside down overnight. I had just found my faith in God and been baptised a few months prior to this tragedy. The nuns were quick to show their support but their guidance didn't feel right – they were asking me to pray also to Mary, because she is the mother of Jesus Christ. I wanted to pray to God – nobody else!

That was the day the Pandora's box opened and inside there were a million questions. Why did my brother die so young? Why was this happening to my family? Why have I been left on my own? How was I going to cope alone? Were my parents going to be okay?

I'm obviously not an exception in losing a relative and we all react in different ways. But Islam has a solution for all. For

1. Cattle, *Surah Al-An'am* (6:98)

Phanou

me, Islam brought light into my heart when it was bursting with grief and sorrow. As Rumi wrote,

"The wound is the place **where the light enters** you."

This couldn't have been truer for me.

Like other monotheistic religions, Islam views death not as the end of our existence but as a new beginning – it is the gateway our soul must pass through in order to live an eternal life. Islam also acknowledges the twofold calamity of both losing loved ones and leaving them behind us.

The Prophet Muhammad assured his followers that, out of death, an eternal house in heaven will arise for those who did well in this world. It promises a better life without suffering, abandonment or sorrow and with no further trials or obligations (even religious); it is a resting house for eternity in which we will be reunited with loved ones and return to our Creator.

Islam teaches us that death goes hand in hand with patience – patience is the tool that God has given us to help us through the initial shock and grief. We must find the courage within us to keep living, which is when patience comes into play: it is the key which fortifies us, helps us deal with grief and overcome it with time – no matter how much time we may need.

Prayer is another powerful tool that gives us spiritual strength – it helps us meditate in calm as our life goes on, it brings us closer to God and helps us accept it as His will. Who else can bring us patience other than God, who describes Himself as *As-Sabur* – 'the Patient One'?

We also are taught not to give up – not to give up on the people who are left behind and for whom we have a responsibility. We must stay strong for the sake of the person who passed away and, most importantly, for those who still need us. Islam always privileges life. Life allows us to keep on honouring those who have passed away – we can still do things for their benefit, such as pray for the forgiveness of their sins, give charity in their name, or perform a pilgrimage on their behalf.

While we are alive, we can also plant seeds which we will continue to harvest and from which we will reap spiritual benefits even once we are in our grave. If, for example, you contribute to building a school, you will be rewarded continuously for the knowledge you are bringing to children. The same goes if you have helped to build a well or a mosque, and so on.

We are encouraged as a community to remember and support those grieving. For a period of three days after a death, friends and neighbours bring food to the bereaved to give them time to mourn.

In Islam, the period of grief is no longer than these three days – of course, this doesn't mean we can't cry after that! The sadness will live in our hearts forever as we will always miss our loved ones. Instead, it simply means that after three days you have to get yourself together and reintegrate into society by going back to work and resuming activities.

There are a few crucial steps in an Islamic funeral:

- While our loved one is on their death bed, it is our duty to help them look forward to meeting their merciful and forgiving Creator, to speak positively and to give them hope for what is to come. An *imam* can come to pray with and for them.
- When he or she passes away, the ritual is to wash their body by having someone perform their major ablutions (*ghusl*). After birth, a newborn baby's body is washed to be presented to the parents; in the same way, we are cleaned and wrapped in white clothes to meet God, for our last and eternal life with Him.
- Women's bodies are wrapped in five pieces of white cloth, including a head scarf, while men's bodies in only three pieces. This is done to respect our human dignity. There are no make-up artists – quite the contrary.
- The majority of Islamic graveyards do not have tombstones with names engraved on them, although in some countries they might be marked by simple headstones for identification.
- Although it's absolutely fine to do so, some people choose not to leave flowers on a grave, as we believe that beyond what the eyes can see, the interior of the grave transforms into a garden of heaven.
- Widows are given a longer grieving period, of four months and ten days, after losing their husband.

Converts are encouraged to leave a will asking their family for an Islamic ritual. As Mufti Menk said, “Nothing is certain in this life except our return to our Maker. Not many want to think about this. Wise is he who prepares for that day”.

Different cultures also have their own traditions to complement the Islamic grieving process.

5. LOVE

When it comes to any relationship in our lives, we must remember that God is number one. It is He who puts love for one another in our hearts and who maintains that love between us.

In Islam, finding our 'better half' is more like finding the 'other half of our faith'. A narration says, "As for he whom Allah provides with a righteous woman, He (Allah) has indeed helped him with half of his religion. Then let him fear Allah with the remaining half."[1] Considering we spend a lifetime as a couple, our relationships should help us grow our spirituality, practice of Islam and knowledge.

In Islam, men are encouraged to look for one specific quality in a wife: her faith. Sure, good looks are important – let's not fool ourselves. But beauty should be a secondary priority. This also applies to women: faith comes first, then his looks, wealth and nobility.

PLAYING MATCH-MAKER

Of course, there's the good old-fashioned way of meeting one another through your own circle of contacts but in many communities you'll also find people keen to set up *halal* 'blind dates'. Usually a mutual relative, friend or colleague will suggest two people meet each other and will give each a bit of background about one another. If both agree, they will meet in the presence of a third person (kind of like a third wheel!). This is a very popular method in many communities, and these recommendations are highly valued by bachelors and bachelorettes. They trust their friends, who have their best interests at heart and know them well. Besides, everyone likes to play match-maker and reap the rewards of creating a happy marriage!

1. Hadith source: Al-Hakim

I've said this before and will say it again because it's a common misconception about Muslims: forced marriages are not allowed in Islam and women have the right to refuse any proposal. There is a narration that says, "A woman whom has been previously married has more right concerning herself than her guardian, and a virgin's consent must be asked about herself..."[1]

A word of warning, there's a frenzy around new Muslims to get them married as soon as possible. I'm not sure why this sudden rush to push two people into taking a lifetime decision – as if embracing a new religion with so much to learn and take on was not enough to deal with.

Marriage is not a matter to be taken lightly under any circumstance, especially at a time of conversion when a new leaf turns and the real adventure begins.

Besides, one should first wrap their head around the rights and obligations of a spouse within an Islamic marriage. For a convert, a cross-cultural marriage might be on the cards. Marrying into another culture with its own traditions is another factor to seriously consider beforehand, as it can hide several bumps down the road that may impact the couple. If this is something you would consider, it would be wise to have a frank discussion about the expectations of your future in-laws. You don't just marry your husband; you marry into a family! Expectations from a mother-in-law in regards to duties or raising your children vary hugely between the West and East for example.

IT'S GETTING SERIOUS (OR NOT)

One of the advantages of getting to know one another through Islam is that each party can enquire about the other. For example, you can speak to a man's sister or an aunt to get an honest (if a little biased!) appraisal, speak to work

1. Hadith source: Bukhari and Muslim

colleagues or contact people in the community that have dealt with him. For a third point of view, you could even speak to people who don't like him if you want to and ask why they feel that way. Of course, this should be done in transparency, respect and in full confidence.

Sexual relations are forbidden before marriage, whether both people are virgins or if they have been married before. Each partner should save themselves for their future spouse, in fact respecting one another's chastity vows forms a very strong bond and trust between the two fiancés. Once married, rest assured a healthy sexual relationship is encouraged in Islam, which views sexual needs as natural and healthy for both the wife and the husband. They are not buried in feelings of guilt, although some societies have adopted a shame-based attitude towards the subject. However, Prophet Muhammad was never shy to discuss this subject openly within the framework of education and to develop closeness and pleasure within a marriage.

If he wants to propose, the tradition encourages men to speak to the bride-to-be's father or mother and ask for their daughter's hand in marriage. Showing respect to the in-laws is a must!

By the way, did you know that women can propose to men in Islam? Did you know that a man can marry an older woman? That a man can marry a divorced woman or a widow?

The poet Kahlil Gibran described relationships beautifully in his poem *On Marriage*.

Let there be spaces in your togetherness,
And let the winds of the heavens dance between you.

Love one another but make not a bond of love:
Let it rather be a moving sea between the shores of your souls.
Fill each other's cup but drink not from one cup. Give one another of your bread but eat not from the same loaf.
Sing and dance together and be joyous, but let each one of you be alone,
Even as the strings of a lute are alone though they quiver with the same music.

Give your hearts, but not into each other's keeping.
For only the hand of Life can contain your hearts.
And stand together, yet not too near together:
For the pillars of the temple stand apart,
And the oak tree and the cypress grow not in each other's shadow.

What I draw from this poem is that it is important to love a man but it is also important to remain your own person; your individuality and differences will enrich each other's lives.

BRIDEZILLAS

If you've said yes to a proposal, bear in mind that the whole process of getting married is fairly simple. First of all, getting engaged simply means that the proposal has been accepted by the couple and by both sides of the family. It's kind of a 'booking', meaning that neither can seek marriage with anybody else. There's no 'open relationship' in Islam! It's the real deal.

Some families choose to have a celebration for the wedding and that's great, as long as you have the financial means to do so. Who wants to start off their married life with debts? The party is not an obligation and it's absolutely fine to keep it low-key.

1. Hadith source: Bukhari

AS FOR THE WEDDING, BRIDEZILLAS REST ASSURED – ISLAMIC WEDDINGS ARE SURPRISINGLY EASY AND BUDGET-FRIENDLY. ALL YOU NEED IS:

1 **A *walee*** – the tutor of the bride, usually her biological or adoptive father, her brother or uncle.

Two male witnesses – they should be trustworthy, with both of your best interests at heart. 2

3 **A dowry.** What is it? It's not how much you're worth because, let's face it, nobody on earth would be able to afford that! While it's perfectly acceptable for the dowry to be a large amount (within reason), it's mainly a symbolic gesture from the groom to the bride only, as a gift for her exclusive use. Even if it's just something small, it will still be accepted. As the Prophet Muhammad said: "Look for one even if it was an iron ring."[1]

Your local mosque – the *imam* invites the whole family to unite the bride and groom to exchange vows. 4

5 **Your townhall** – seal the deal officially by getting a legally binding marriage certificate. *Imams* in non-Muslim countries will not usually accept a wedding unless it is first recognised by the law of your country.

Last but not least, don't be afraid to discuss a marriage contract with your beau. At this point in the relationship, details are meant to be discussed and mutually agreed upon.

A contract is a means of protection for both individuals and by signing it, you both agree to give the other their rights. Where its terms are not respected, someone will be held accountable to God and by law.

Islam encourages us to be realistic towards the situations that life throws at us; my dad likes to play the role of the 'devil's advocate' as he likes to put it, to help me weigh the pros and cons. Islam also encourages us to take an unsentimental approach for important decisions and recognises that as human beings, we have shortcomings. Having a clear agreement before marriage of the expectations we have for one another will avoid a great deal of heartache and confusion, don't you agree? It's actually comforting to know we have safeguards in place and where we're headed. This does not mean that the marriage is just a contractual burden, empty of love and romance, on the contrary the couple can work on building a strong emotional bond with each other once this is out of the way.

If, for one reason or another, your fiancé is not transparent with one or more of the above points, figure out why as there may be something fishy. You shouldn't be hidden from his family and your parents should be aware that you are married; it's a once-in-a-lifetime celebration and it needs to be official. From one sister to another, I am warning you against some of the brothers out there and asking you to be vigilant! Follow your heart, trust your gut and use your head.

DIVORCE

There are a lot of misunderstandings around Muslim divorce. We all hope our marriage will not come to that but sometimes it's inevitable, and for the best.

The way that divorce is described in the Quran is very positive and respectful; unfortunately, these days it is rare to find couples who apply this attitude and it can get ugly, hurting children for life in the process. When the man wants a divorce:

- Every divorce comes from a problem or misunderstanding. The first step is to pinpoint the misunderstandings and to help the couple overcome them so that they can be reconciled. This is done by seeking an intervention, using one representative from each side of the family as mediators, to find a solution.
- If the man still wants to proceed with the divorce, the next step is to continue to live with his wife for approximately three months (more precisely, three menstrual cycles). He shall actively participate in the household and even continue to sleep in the same bed as his wife – but the key is not to engage in any kind of sexual relations, unless he wants to reconcile and abandon the divorce.
- Once the three cycles are over, he should pronounce the divorce for a second time (unless he now wishes to stay married). Then, once again, the man should live with his wife for another three cycles.
- At the end of the sixth cycle, he is asked if he still wants to proceed. If, at any point during the six cycles, the man has had sexual relations with his wife, the whole process is cancelled.
- If he still can't make up his mind, his wife is allowed to leave immediately.
- The divorce is valid once the courts declare the divorce.
- In any case, the man shall continue to give spousal maintenance to his wife. The amount is decided case by case depending on her living conditions.

When the woman seeks a divorce, she and her lawyer can take action immediately, and this will be recognised by *imams*.

Although divorce is allowed in Islam, the process is designed to make sure that the couple aren't acting in the heat of the moment. It gives them time to take a breather and re-think the situation from a distance.

Living in the same house and sleeping side by side could make couples reconsider their decision if there is a spark of love left within their hearts. This trial could even help them to deepen their love and rekindle their relationship afresh. Every couple confronts life and its ups and downs for the better and the worst during their journey.

The opposite is also true: if no love remains, then spending your last few months with one another might at least help you to close your relationship with respect and dignity. It will also give you time to plan the transition and organise your new life, especially beneficial if you have kids together.

However, if your partner is violent and puts your life in danger, there is absolutely no obligation for you to share the same home, let alone the same bed. You can stay at your parents' house or with a friend until the divorce is finalised.

6. PARTING WORDS

The *ummah* is an intricate spider web that connects both people born into Islam and those who find Islam at some point later in their life. As Mufti Menk puts it, "Don't think being 'religious' means becoming harsh or hard. When Allah enters a heart, He softens it, He doesn't harden it."

Finding peace will bring solace to your heart. Every person comes with their own nature – change your bad habits but keep the good ones! You will stay 'you'; you will simply benefit from the process as you make positive changes to your way of thinking. Think of it like adding more sprinkles to the top of the cupcake!

Becoming a Muslim can be a really emotional time; it can be exhilarating, liberating, challenging, scary, confusing, exciting, nerve-wracking… Everyone's experience is completely unique. One thing is universal, though: it's a time of transformation, so it's important to try to remain calm and not let all the new information and changes overwhelm you. My parting advice for you as a new Muslim would be to take things on gradually and at your own pace. After all, this is a new way of life, not just a new chapter. Don't force what may seem unnatural at first – do what makes sense to you and question what doesn't until you understand the logic.

You know yourself better than anyone. People with good intentions will come from all sides trying to advise you. While it's always good to be receptive to advice, to learn more and understand different perspectives, don't let anyone push you into doing things you're not ready to do. Remember to watch out for the difference between the teachings of our Prophet and simply cultural customs. Be confident in what you are learning.

REVERTING: A LEAP OF FAITH

The preferred term for referring to a new Muslim is not 'convert' but 'revert'. Why? Prophet Muhammad said:

> "Every child is born
> on the natural inclination of 'Islam'[1]
> (meaning surrender, submission to God)."

Growing up, our upbringing diverts us from this inclination. We believe that when we embrace Islam, we return to this natural state – hence we 'revert' to Islam.

I'll never forget walking to class in high school after becoming Muslim when a Christian classmate sadly said, "You made Jesus cry".

My reaction? I smiled. Not because I was mocking my classmate, but because deep inside I've always felt like Islam is the accomplishment of my years of soul-searching for the truth, an essential piece of the puzzle in my journey of faith and a continuation of my growth in knowledge.

Christianity took me a step closer to Islam and taught me the stories of our Prophets, as well as values that I will forever cherish – love, compassion, forgiveness. Since reverting to Islam, I have never once felt that I left Christianity behind or denied the existence of Jesus. On the contrary, Islam reveals the truth behind his story.

1. Hadith source: Al-Hakim

So, I smiled at my classmate because I was taken aback, but also because I knew that my belief in Jesus as one of the Messengers of God had been reinforced and had taken me a step closer to finding my true self – a Muslim.

Although I felt the same after saying my *shahada*, these types of comments made me acknowledge that I was 'different' now – and I was really proud of having taken a leap of faith! We are all unique and should be different.

I didn't meet other converts for years after my own conversion. In the meantime, I would read these words, written by the Mexican painter Frida Kahlo: "I used to think I was the strangest person in the world but then I thought there are so many people in the world, there must be someone just like me who feels bizarre and flawed in the same ways I do. I would imagine her, and imagine that she must be out there thinking of me, too. Well, I hope that if you are out there and read this and know that, yes, it's true I'm here, and I'm just as strange as you."

If you feel this way too, know that there are other women out there just like you!

Last but not least, at some point in your life you should let your loved ones know that you are a Muslim. Even if they don't react well initially, with time they will come around and ask questions. As long as you are there for them and you show your kindness and all the positive changes Islam has brought to your life, they should learn to accept your decision and live with it, even if they don't agree. How many stories have I heard of people converting after dozens of years – my mum being the living proof!

Also, it is important to find a sincere and devoted *imam* and a mosque – these will be your spiritual guidance throughout your journey. It is helpful to have one person to answer your questions one-on-one, rather than scrabbling for confusing answers online with 'Sheikh' Google.

FINDING YOUR MUSLIM NAME

Changing your name isn't obligatory at all and is completely up to you. If you feel like you want to adopt an 'Islamic' name – one with a good meaning – then you can by all means find a new name for yourself. This is highly recommended if your name has a negative meaning. For example, we spoke about Malcolm X earlier – his birth name was Malcolm Little, which was a slave name with a negative connotation. That's why he changed it to Malcolm X, and later to Malik El-Shabazz.

Personally, I was eighteen years old when I embraced Islam and felt excited to choose a new name. I picked Loujayne, a traditional Omani Muslim name meaning 'silver' (quite fitting as my father was a jeweller!). Now I carry a part of some of my happiest childhood memories everywhere I go – but most of all, it symbolises the ideal Muslim woman I want to be. With the name in mind, I mentally drew a picture of who I was hoping to become on my spiritual journey. This helped me combine two intricate parts of my identity – on one hand, my values and education; on the other, my spiritual self, Loujayne.

Even though I didn't legally change my name and my parents will always call me by my birth name, I like to be addressed as Loujayne by other Muslims.

Arabic names all have a meaning, so you can pick one from the wives or daughters of Prophet Muhammad, or feminine words that are mentioned in the Quran. You can look up lists of names and their meanings online. A friend of mine wasn't sure if she wanted an Islamic name until, one day, we attended a class together at the Islamic centre in which they analysed the description of God as mentioned in a chapter of the Quran called 'The Light' (*Surah An-Noor*).

My friend is a photographer and has an artistic talent for looking at beauty through discerning eyes. Her new name clicked, right there and then: Noor (Arabic for 'light') is profound, indescribable; without it she could not create her art and express herself.

CONVERSION CERTIFICATE

Obtaining a conversion certificate isn't essential but getting one from your mosque or Islamic centre can be helpful to prove to the authorities that you are Muslim, especially if you want to travel for *hajj* and *umrah*, or for when you get married.

Returning the favour: helping out new Muslims

If you're in a situation where a friend or colleague comes to you with questions, I encourage you to take this person under your wing as best you can, whether you direct them to the best person to help or decide to teach them to the best of your knowledge. This can be a life-changing and inspirational experience for you, too, as you witness this person's transition into becoming a Muslim. We all learn from one another in this world. Prophet Muhammad has said that "the happy person is the one who takes lessons from other people."[1]

As you know from your own experience, becoming a Muslim is simple. All they have to do is pronounce the *shahada*, bearing witness that there is no God but Allah and that the Prophet Muhammad is His messenger. You can explain to them that they can do this in the presence of at least two Muslims or, if possible, at the mosque. The mosque is always a good idea as establishing a link with it can help them become part of their local Muslim community. If they have no Muslims in their area, or if you don't know of any,

1. Hadith source: Al-Hakim

they can say the *shahada* out loud with God as their witness. However, try to encourage them to visit a mosque or Islamic centre as soon as possible so that they're not alone. They will benefit hugely from being in touch with people who can help them and support them.

My mother-in-law regularly meets new women who come to her Sunday *halaqas* for the first time, on the verge of embracing Islam. At this stage, they usually have a few burning questions on their minds, want to get to know the community, understand the lifestyle and feel reassured that they are making the right decision. So, she created a buddy program which ensures that these women are accompanied in their journey by one of her regular students after their *shahada* – the testimony of faith and first pillar in Islam. It was so heart-warming for me to meet some of the beautiful friendships that have been created as a result!

Likewise, I have witnessed a few close friends embracing Islam. Those moments have been some of the most treasured highlights of my life. They bring a new dimension to a friendship and you feel the love that Allah amplifies in our hearts.

If you are up for it, you could also take a course at your Islamic centre on how to give *dawah* (meaning how to invite others to Islam).

SPREAD THE LIGHT AROUND LIKE GLITTER

God beautifully describes the status of non-believers in the chapter 'The Light' (one of the names and attributes of God):

"Or else, like the depths of darkness in a vast deep ocean, covered by waves above which are waves, with clouds above it all: depths of darkness, layer upon layer, [so that] when one holds up his hand, he can hardly see it. Indeed the one from whom God withholds light shall find no light at all."[2]

When you embraced Islam, you probably felt the urge to shout it on the rooftops, and especially with your family. But they might not have been so welcoming to the idea and, I'm not going to lie, it can be really frustrating.

I think the most difficult verse from the Quran for me and other reverts is the following:

> "Indeed, you cannot guide aright everyone whom you love. **It is God who guides whom He wills.** He knows best those who are guided aright.[3]"

We can't force anyone to do anything in Islam, let alone force someone to become a Muslim. In fact, the Quran tells us, "There shall be no compulsion in religion. The right way is henceforth distinct from error. He who rejects false deities and believes in God has indeed taken hold of a most firm support that never breaks. God hears all and knows all."[4]

While we hope that our children, parents, brothers, sisters and friends will research Islam, read the Quran, believe in

2. Light, *Surah An-Noor* (24:40)

3. The Story, *Surah Al-Qasas* (28:56)

4. The Cow, *Surah Al-Baqarah* (2:256)

the Prophet Muhammad, and say their testimony of faith, it is He who guides whom He wills – end of story. We must simply pray to Allah to keep us on His straight path, to help us spread His message of truth and to guide and protect our loves ones.

Having said that, we shouldn't give up all hope.

In fact, I initially got the idea of writing this book in 2009. Back then, I wanted to write it for my mum. My father and I had both converted to Islam and I was so eager for my mum to join us and become a Muslim too. I wanted to share with her all the beautiful things I had discovered through my journey. I am really grateful that God didn't wait the nine years it took me to finish writing this book before my mum became a Muslim!

I hope that in sharing my journey with you, you will kick-start your new way of life: only you hold the keys to continue your spiritual journey. Hopefully, through reading these chapters you have learnt that seeking knowledge and steady self-progress are some of the most important tools to living a balanced lifestyle as a new Muslim; that the five pillars will be the foundation to your faith; that prayer will lead you to success; and charitable acts will connect you with the world.

Beyond a stronger faith, I hope that you have gained a clearer mind, a brighter heart and a thirst to continue learning.

This global sisterhood of women is waiting to welcome you. Discover your nearby mosque and Muslim community, find like-minded sisters who will continue to inspire you.

You have the opportunity to take those steps to become your true self, the best person you can be, to reach your fullest potential. Look after your faith, care for yourself and others, and brighten your inner light! ■

“

Were all the trees on earth made into pens, and the sea ink, with seven more seas yet added to it, the Words of God would not be exhausted. God is indeed Almighty, All-Wise.[1]

”

1. Luqman (31:27)

TERMINOLOGY

Term	Meaning
A'udhu billahi min ash-shaytaan ir-rajeem	I seek God's protection against Satan, the accursed one
Abaya	A full-length outer garment worn by some modest Muslim women
Adhan	Call to prayer
Aisha	Wife of Prophet Muhammad
Ajwa	Blessed dates from Madinah, Kingdom of Saudi Arabia
Al Fatihah	The first *surah* of the Quran, meaning 'The Opener'
Alayhi Salaam (AS)	For all prophets and messengers of God, as well as the Archangel Gabriel, Muslims say 'peace be upon him'
Alhamdulillah	Praise be to Allah
Allah	Literally translates to 'The God' – 'the' emphasising that there is no other.
Allahu Akbar	God is the Greatest
Asiya	Wife of the Pharaoh, also known as *Bithiah* in biblical texts
Asr	Third prayer of the day, when the shadow of any object stretches to 1.5 times its original length
As-Salaamu alaikum	Greetings of salutation – meaning: 'may peace be upon you'

Astaghfirullah	I seek forgiveness from Allah
Ayat	Each chapter of the Quran is divided into numbered verses (*ayat* in plural form). Literally means ‘a sign’ of God’s miracles
Bismillah	‘In the name of God’. We invoke God by His name whenever we are about to start something so that we can gain His blessing
Bismillah alRahman alRaheem	In the name of God, the Most Gracious, the Most Merciful. All *Surahs*, with the exception of one, begin with this formula
Burka	A long, loose garment covering the whole body from head to feet
Burkini	Modest swimwear for Muslim women
Dars	Islamic class or lesson
Dawah	Inviting others to Islam
Dawud	Prophet David
Deen	Islam’s complete way of life
Dhikr	Considered as a form of devotion, literally meaning ‘to remember’. It helps us become closer to God by remembering Him
Dhuhr	Second prayer of the day when the sun begins to decline after reaching its highest point in the sky
Dua	Prayer said as an invocation or supplication
Eid	Celebration
Eid al-Adha	The ‘Sacrifice feast’ and the holiest of the two annual *Eids* as it commemorates Prophet Abraham’s great sacrifice

Eid al-fitr	Celebration that marks the end of the holy month of Ramadan
Eid Mubarak	A greeting meaning 'Happy *Eid*'
Fajr	Pre-dawn prayer
Fatima	Daughter of Prophet Mohammad, also known as *'az-Zahra'* (the splendid and radiant one)
Fatwa	A ruling issued by a scholar
Fiqh	Islamic jurisprudence
Ghusl	Mandatory bath and major ablutions (full body washing)
Hadith	Sayings of Prophet Muhammad which have been recorded and passed down the generations
Hajar	The mother of Prophet *Ishmael* and second wife of Prophet Abraham, also known as *Hagar*
Hajj	Fifth pillar of Islam – the major pilgrimage performed during the twelfth and final month of the lunar calendar. Muslims are obligated to perform *Hajj* once in their lifetime, provided they have the financial means to do so and are physically fit
Hajjah	Title of respect for a woman who has perfomed the greater pilgrimage, *Hajj*, the fifth pillar of Islam
Halal	What is made permissible in Islam
Halaqa	A religious talk; a circle of knowledge
Haram	What is not permissible, forbidden, in Islam. Depending on the pronunciation, it can also

	mean 'sanctuary' or 'sacred' such as Masjid al-Haram (Sacred Mosque in Mecca, Saudi Arabia)
Hasan and Husain	Grandsons of Prophet Muhammad: sons of his daughter Fatima and Ali. They are the leaders of the youth in Paradise
Hayya	Modesty
Henna	A natural orange/brown dye which is applied directly on the skin and nails and gradually fades after a few days. Popular at weddings and *Eid*
Hijab	Islamic veil; a way to connect with Allah and guard one's modesty
Hijama	Cupping performed on specific spots on the body
Hind (Umm Salama)	Wife of Prophet Muhammad
Hira	Cave of Hira in the Mountain of Light (*Jabal al-Noor*), where the Quran was revealed to Prophet Muhammad
Iblis	Satan
Ibrahim	Prophet Abraham, who built the Holy Kaaba with his son *Ishmael*
Idris	Prophet Enoch
Iftar	The meal that breaks fast at sunset (also called *futoor*)
Imam	Religious leader of the Muslim community at the mosque
Iman	Faith
InshaAllah	God willing

Iqamah	Second call to prayer after the *adhan*
Isha	Fifth and last prayer of the day, when darkness falls and there is no scattered light in the sky
Ishaaq	Prophet Isaac, son of Prophet Abraham and Sarah and brother to Ishmael
Islam	Derived from the Arabic root '*saalam*', meaning 'peace'.
Ismail	Prophet Ishmael, son of Prophet Abraham and Hajar and brother to Isaac. Ancestor of Prophet Muhammad
Isra Wal Miraj	The night journey (*isra*) that Prophet Muhammad took from Mecca to Jerusalem and his ascension (*miraj*) through the spheres of Heaven
Issa	Jesus, the Prophet and Messenger of God, son of Maryam (the Virgin Mary)
Itikaf	A full immersion of several days dedicated to prayer at the mosque, during the Holy month of Ramadan
Jabal al-Noor	Mountain of Light where the Quran was first revealed to Prophet Muhammad in the Cave of Hira (Mecca, Saudi Arabia)
Jerusalem	Capital city of Palestine, where Masjid Al-Aqsa is located
Jibrail	Archangel Gabriel
Jihad	Meaning an 'effort', of which two types are mentioned: the greater and lesser *jihad*
Jinn	Genie, created before man from the smokeless flame of fire
Kaaba	'House of God' built by Prophet Abraham with his son Ishmael located in Masjid al-Haram (Mecca, Saudi Arabia).

Khadijah	First wife of Prophet Mohammad
Khutbah	Sermon made by an *imam*
Laylat al-qadr	The night of Power and Decree when the Holy Quran was revealed. Takes place in the last ten days of the Holy month of Ramadan
Maghrib	Fourth prayer of the day, at sunset
Maryam	Virgin Mary, mother of Prophet Jesus
Masjid	Mosque
Masjid Al-Aqsa	Al-Aqsa Mosque, the third holiest site in Islam, located in the Old City of Jerusalem
Masjid Al-Haram	Grand Mosque of Mecca, the largest mosque in the world, which houses the Holy Kaaba (Kingdom of Saudi Arabia)
Masjid an-Nabawi	Prophet Mohammad's mosque in Medina, Saudi Arabia
Mecca	The holiest city in Islam, where the Holy Kaaba is located (Saudi Arabia)
Medina	The second holiest city in Islam, where Masjid an-Nabawi is located
Mihrab	A niche in the wall of a mosque that indicates the direction of the Holy Kaaba
Minbar	The pulpit inside the mosque from which the *imam* conducts the sermons
Miswak	A twig with a frayed end used to clean teeth
Muezzin	Man who recites the call to prayer to be heard outdoor
Musa	Prophet Moses

Musalla	Prayer space in a mosque or outdoors where *Eid* prayers are performed
Mus-haf	Quran written in Arabic
Niqab	Full-face veil
Noor	Light; also the twenty-fourth *Surah* of the Quran; and *'an-Noor'* – one of the 99 names and attributes of Allah (The Light)
Nuh	Prophet Noah
Qibla	The direction, toward the Kaaba in Mecca, which all Muslims face to pray *salah* five times a day
Qiyam al-layl	The prayer that takes place in the middle of the night during the last ten days of Ramadan
Quran	The name of Islam's sacred book, which has remained authentic and true to its original form since God revealed it. Derived from Arabic words for 'to collect' (*al-Qar*) and 'to recite' (*Qara*).
Radi Allah 'Anha/Anhu (RA)	Muslims pay their respect to Prophet Mohammad's wives and companions by saying, 'May Allah be pleased with her/him' (*'Anha* for a female companion, or *'Anhu* for a male)
Ramadan	Ninth month of the Islamic lunar calendar, when Muslims around the world fast to fulfil one of the pillars of Islam
Ruqayyah	Daughter of Prophet Muhammad
Ruqyah	Method of natural healing through prayer
Sadaqa	Voluntary charity
Saee	Pilgrimage ritual to commemorate Hajar's journey from mount Safwa and Marwa
Safa and Marwa	The two hilltops between which Muslims run back and forth seven times in their pilgrimage, to commemorate the footsteps of Hajar (*Saee*)

Sahabah	Companions of Prophet Mohammad, including his family members
Salaam	Peace
Salah	Second pillar of Islam – the obligatory, ritual prayer which we do five times a day at prescribed timings
Salat al-istikhara	The Guidance Prayer
Sall Allahu Alay-hi wa-sallam (SAW)	Wishing Prophet Muhammad 'peace and blessings be upon him' (also abbreviated as PBUH)
Sawm	The fourth pillar of Islam – fasting
Shahada	First pillar of Islam – the first step to 'officially' become Muslim with God as a witness by pronouncing the testimony of faith: 'There is no god but Allah. Muhammad is the messenger of God'
Sharia	Religious law derived from the precept of Islam, particulary the Holy Quran and the *Hadith*
Sheikh	Islamic scholar with jurisprudence knowledge
Siwaak	A twig with a frayed end used to clean teeth
SubhanAllah	Glory be to Allah
Suhoor	Morning meal before fasting during Ramadan, eaten before dawn
Sujood	The act of putting your head down on the ground between your hands; one of the positions performed in *Salah*
Sunnah	Actions of Prophet Muhammad which have been recorded and passed down the generations, a guide for Muslims to follow with the Prophet Muhammad as our example

Surah	Chapter of the Quran
Tafseer	Interpretation of the Quran
Tajweed	The practice of reciting the Quran with correct pronunciation
Taqabal Allah wa minkum	'May Allah accept (this worship) from you and us' – usually said to another worshipper after a prayer
Taraweh	A prayer performed daily at the mosque during Ramadan straight after the night prayer, *Isha*. This starts the night before the first day of fasting and then takes place all month
Tasbeeh	Prayer beads or special clickers used for *dhikr* (remembering Allah)
Ummah	The whole community of Muslims bound together by ties of religion
Umrah	The lesser pilgrimage (*hajj* is the major pilgrimage), which is recommended but not compulsory and can be performed at any time
Wa alaykum as-salaam	A reply to greetings of peace, meaning 'and peace unto you'
Wa alaykum as-salaam wa rahmatullahu wa barakatuhu	A reply to greetings of peace, meaning 'and may the peace, mercy and blessings of God be with you'
Walee	The tutor of the bride, usually her biological or adoptive father, her brother or uncle
Wudhu	Minor ablutions, a cleanliness ritual performed before prayer
Yaqub	Prophet Jacob, father of Prophet Yusuf
Yusuf	Prophet Joseph, son of Prophet Yaqub

Zakah	Third pillar of Islam – social welfare tax. Literally means 'purification' because it's a way for Muslims to purify their wealth and their heart
Zakat al-fitr	Before the *Eid* prayer it is a duty upon every Muslim family to pay a charity to the poor, the equivalent of about 2kg of flour, wheat, barley or rice
Zamzam	Holy and blessed water that has many virtues and is said to be a food that nourishes. Its source is in Makkah, Saudi Arabia and still flows today

REFERENCES

Book title	Author	Publisher
The Fortress of the Muslim		Darussalam
Muhammad: His Life Based on the Earliest Sources	**Martin Lings**	Digital Deen Publiscations
Taking Charge of Your Fertility - The Definitive Guide to Natural Birth Control, Pregnancy Achievement, and Reproductive Health	**Tori Weschler**	Vermilion
From MTV to Mecca - How Islam Inspired My Life	**Kristiane Backer**	Arcadia Books Ltd and Awakening Publications
Bent Rib - A Journey Through Women's Issues in Islam	**Huda Khattab**	International Islamic Publishing House
The Life of the Last Prophet	**Yusuf Islam**	Darussalam
Great Women of Islam - Who Were Given the Good News of Paradise	**Mahmood Ahmad Ghadanfar**	Darussalam
Love of Allah - Experience the Beauty of Salah	**Mishari al-Kharraz**	The Qur'an Projet
1001 Inventions: The Enduring Legacy of Muslim Civilization	**The Foundation for Science Technology and Civilization (fstc)**	National Geographic
Women in the Quran: An Emancipatory Reading	**Asma Lambaret and Myriam Francois-Cerrah**	Kube Publishing Ltd
My Du'a Book	**Abdul Malik Mujahid**	Darussalam

The Qur'an in Plain English	**Iman Torres-Al Haneef**	The Islamic Foundation
Golden Supplications for Children	**Abdul Malik Mujahid**	Darussalam
Mathilde a Loinbourg	**Anne Bruneteaux**	Sagesse d'Orient
Generation M: Young Muslims Changing the World	**Shelina Janmohamed**	I.B. Tauris
'Aisha Epouse du Prophete ou L'Islam au Feminin	**Asma Lamrabet**	Tawhid
Reclaim Your Heart	**Yasmin Mogahed**	FB Publishing
Fighting Hislam: Women, Faith and Sexism	**Dr Susan Carland**	ReadHowYouWant
Motivational Moments	**Mufti Ismail Menk**	ALQ Creative
Life of an Outlaw	**Mutah Beale**	
Diam's autobiographie	**Mélanie Georgiades**	Don quichotte
Childhood Champions	**George Green**	Echo Books
Understanding the Qur'an	**Muhammad Abdel Haleem**	I.B.Tauris
Healing with the Medicine of the Prophet	**Ibn Qayyim al-Jawziyya**	Darussalam
Don't be Sad	**'A'id Qurani**	International Islamic Publishing House
From My Sisters' Lips	**Na'ima Roberts**	Bantam Press

www.Quran.com

www.Sunnah.com

INDEX